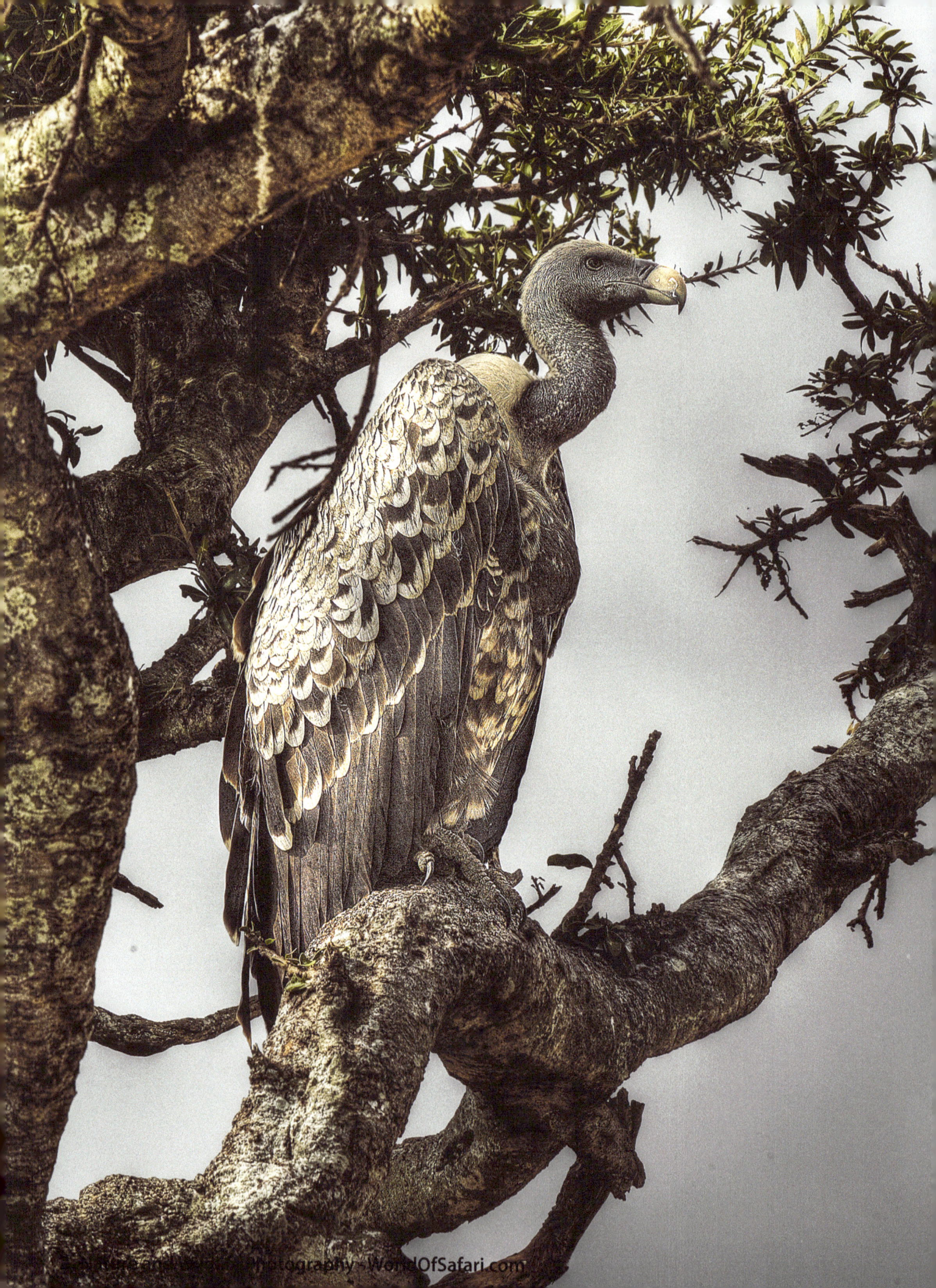

COPYRIGHT INFORMATION

Copyright 2013 by Martin Prüss
www.WorldOfSafari.com

Photographs and text: Martin Prüss

Editor: Sabrina Spangsdorf

Puslihed by Acacian Tales

All product names and services identified in this book are trademarks or registered trademarks of their respective companies. They are used in editorial fashion only and no use of any trade name is intended to convey endorsement or other affiliation with this book.

All rights reserved. No part of this publication may be reproduced, transmitted or stored in any form or by any means – photographic, electronic, mechanical, recorded, photocopied or otherwise, without prior written permission from the publisher.

The author and the publisher have taken all reasonable care in preparing this book. The information contained in this book is based on the author's experience and opinions. We make no warranty about the accuracy or completeness of its content, and to maximum extent permitted, disclaim all liability arising from its use.

EXPOSURE LIKE A PRO

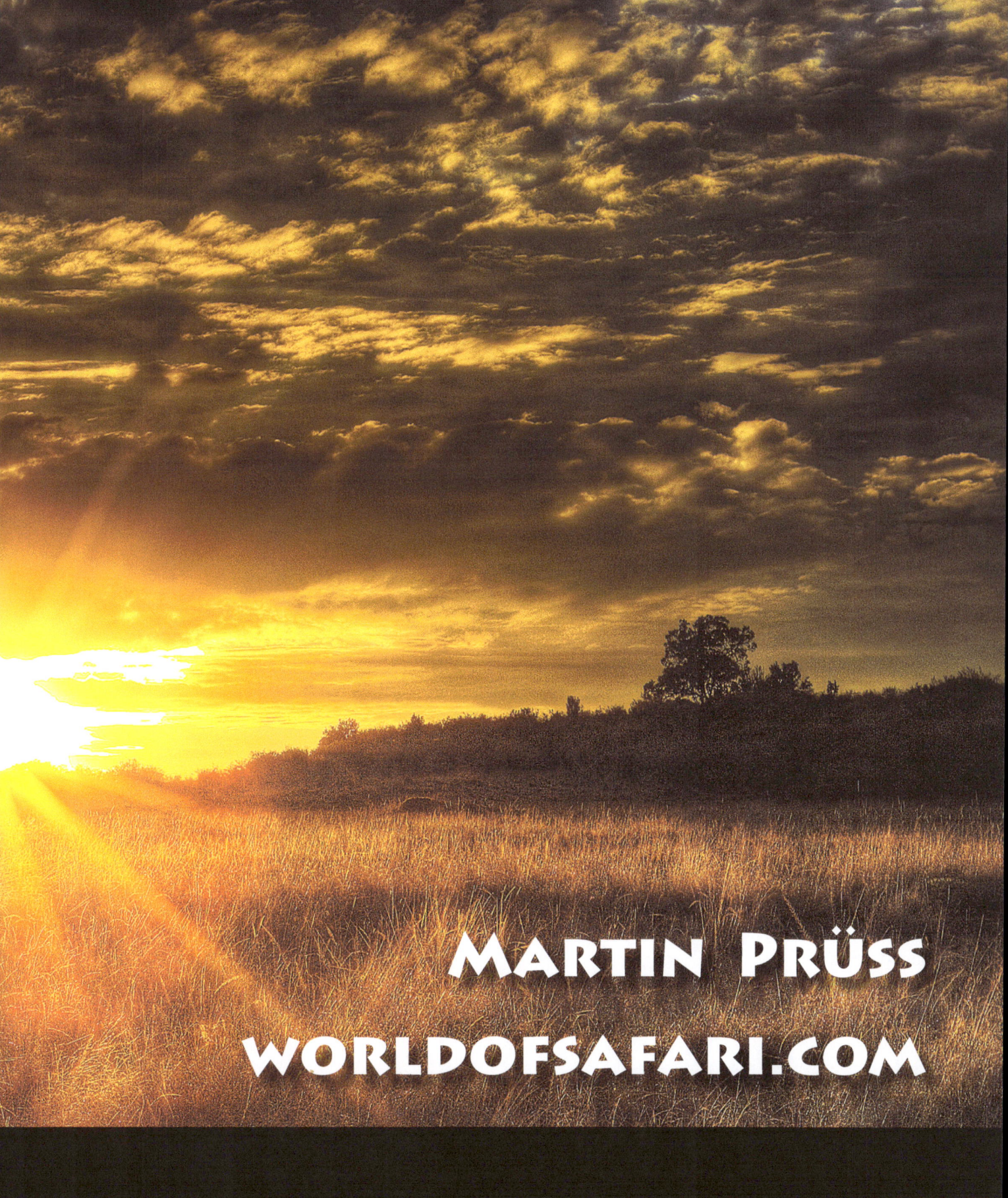

FOREWORD

Wildlife photography is something that comes from your heart and not your head. It requires that you know how to operate your equipment and have the basic skill of photography. Learning the tips and tricks of pros you will be able to capture beautiful wildlife and unique moments in your photographs that last a life time.

In this book I strive to teach you the skills, tips and tricks that can improve your photography skills when photographing wildlife in Africa. The teaching in this book does not only apply to Africa but to general wildlife photography. The book is, however, concentrating on providing you with specific skills needed when photographing wildlife on the African savanna.

As quoted by Karen Blixen the famous Danish author as she described Africa:

"There is something about safari life that makes you forget all your sorrows and feel as if you had drunk half a bottle of champagne - bubbling over with heartfelt gratitude for being alive. One only feels really free when one can go in whatever direction one pleases over the plains, to get to the river at sundown and pitch one's camp, with the knowledge that one can fall asleep beneath other trees, with another view before one, the next night." -Karen Blixen

A special thanks goes to Samuel Ndungu from Somak Safaris, his guidance made many of my wildlife encounters and special moments possible. He taught me the patience needed in the wild to get the best wildlife experiences on a daily basis.

A special thanks to my editor Sabrina Spangsdorf for having patience with me, for guidance in structuring, topics and keeping focus when needed.

Yours sincerely

Martin Prüss

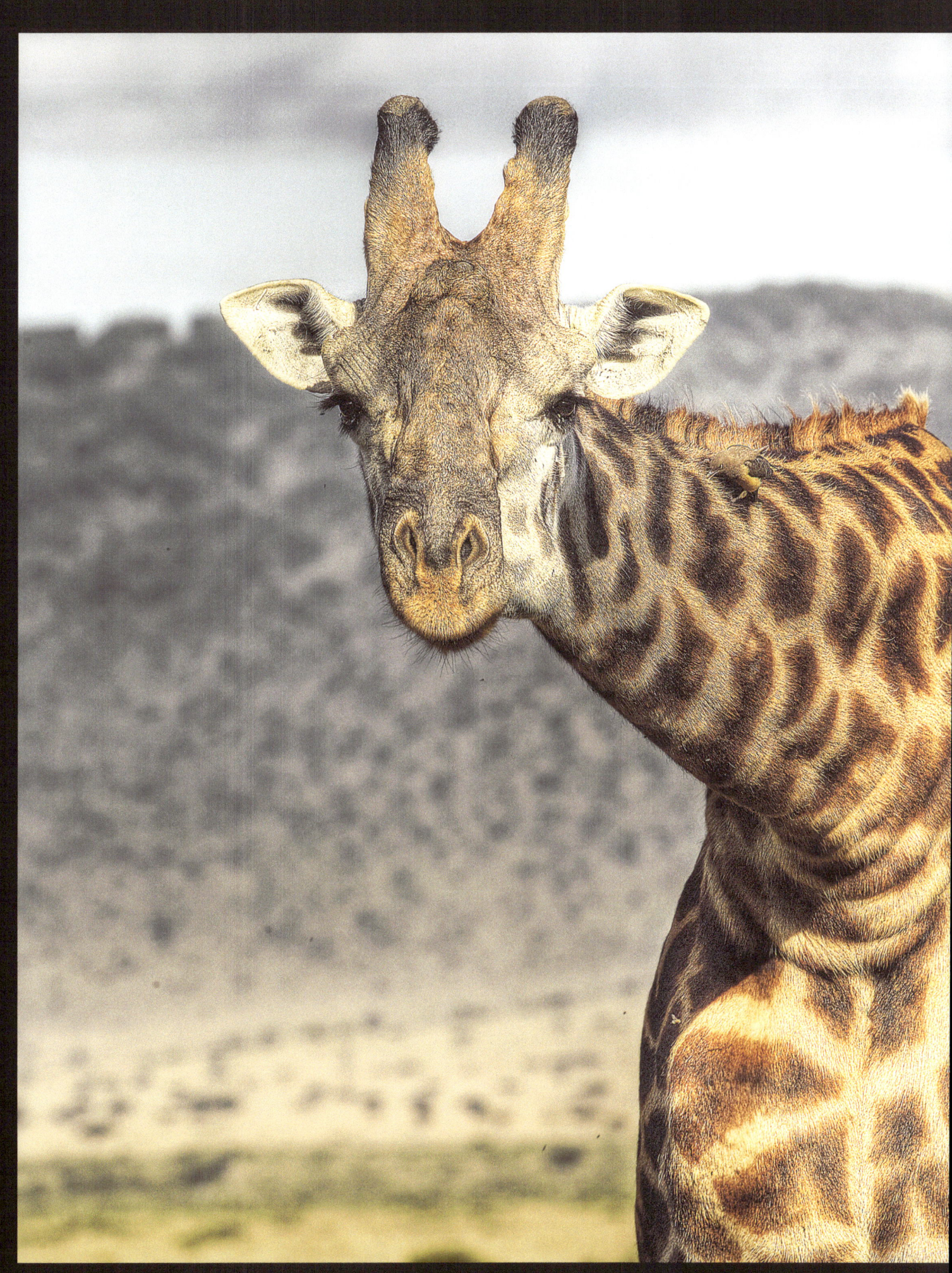

CONTENTS

COPYRIGHT INFORMATION	3
FOREWORD	6
INTRODUCTION	11

THE RIGHT MODE LIKE A PRO — 12

Full Auto	14
Program	17
Aperture priority	18
Shutter priority	20
Manual	22

EXPOSURE LIKE A PRO — 24

ISO	28
Metering light	30
Exposure compensation	33
The sunny 16 rule	36
Bracketing	38
Histogram	41
Exposure problems	44

MORE INFORMATION — 48

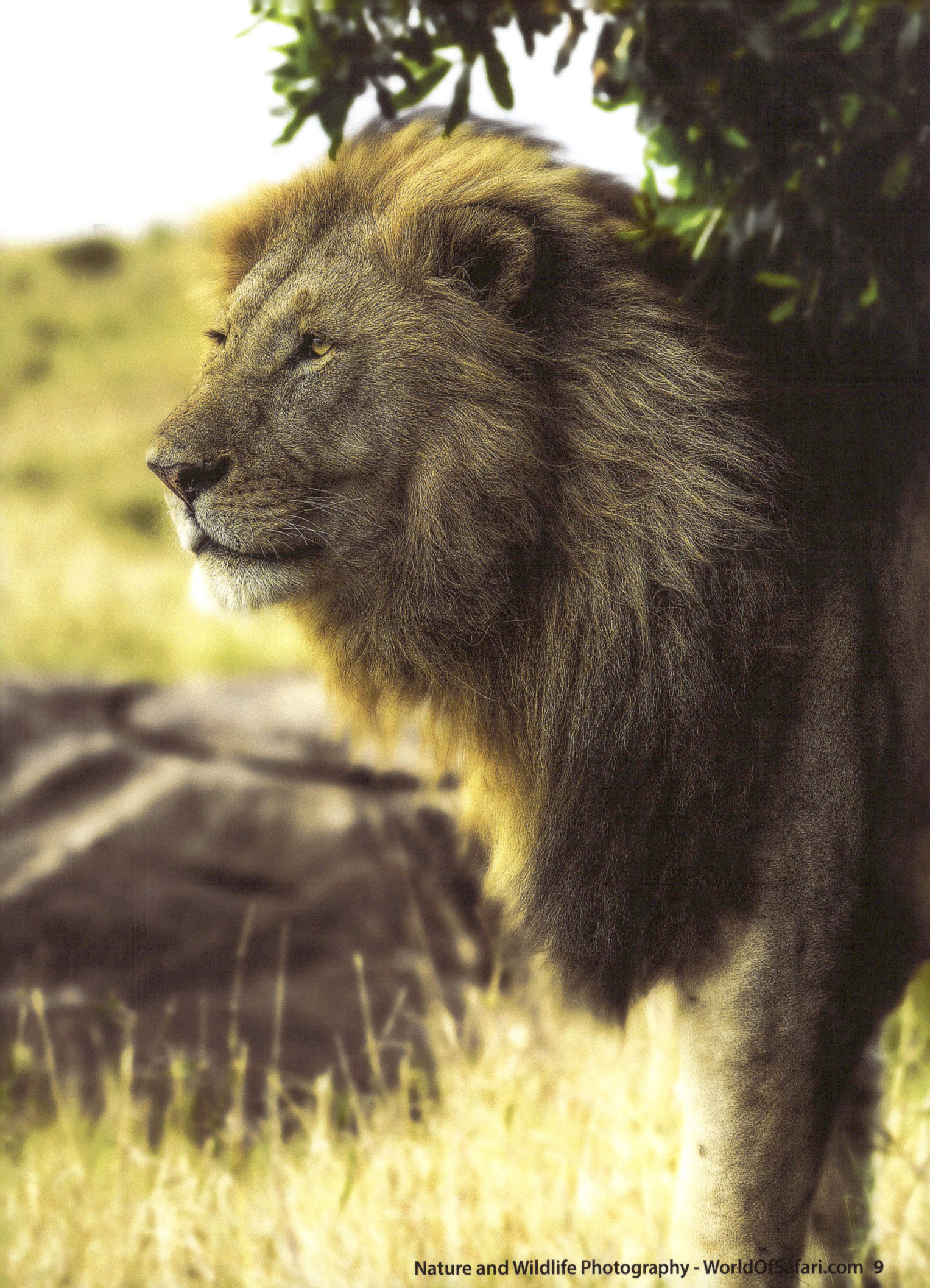

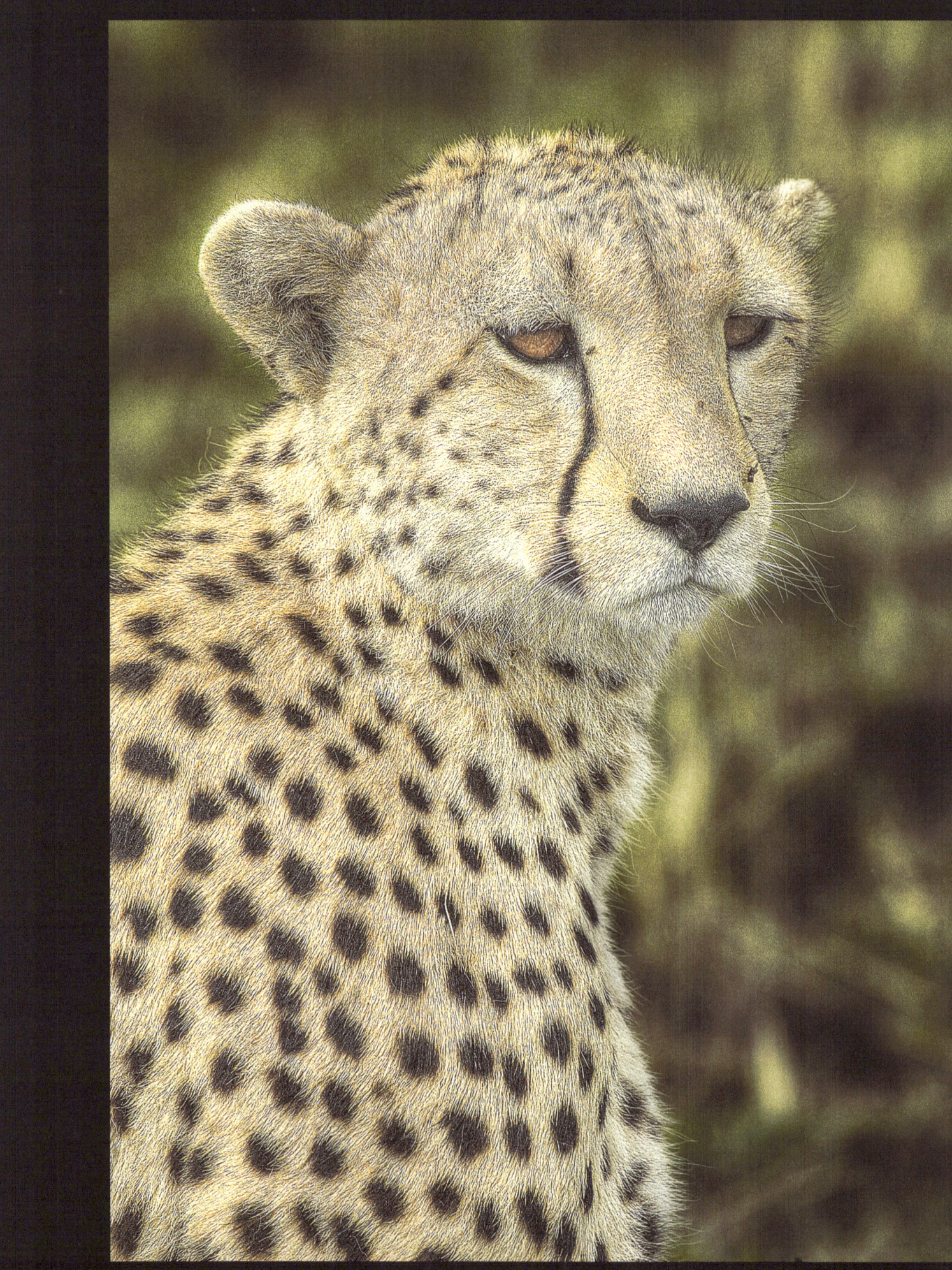

INTRODUCTION

An African safari is a once in a life time experience that captivates and inspires people around the world. Going on a safari in Africa is a breath-taking experience that will stay with you for the rest of your life. From photographers to naturalists a journey to the continent of Africa going on safari creates new memories from day to day, and coming back year after year keeps growing on you. An African safari is the most ultimate photographic experience that I have ever experienced in my travel around the world.

An African safari also reminds you of the importance of conservation and the hard work that wildlife services and related organizations are doing on a daily basis to help protect the wildlife and natural environments for generations to come.

This book is for anyone who has an interest in photography and safari from beginners to semi-professionals striving to get the most from an African safari capturing wildlife photographs that lasts a life time.

All the photographs in this book are from Kenya more specifically the Masai Mara in the south western part at the border to Tanzania and the Serengetti. Masai Mara is to me one of the best places on earth to photograph wildlife and especially the big cats. Masai Mara has the highest concentration of big cats per square kilometer and it is possible to get close to wildlife within its natural habitat.

The techniques, tips and tricks in this book is not just for photographing wildlife in East Africa, but can also be used to photograph wildlife around the world. I have provided specific tips and tricks from my experience in East Africa on how to get the most out of a photo safari in Kenya or Tanzania.

I hope that you can use this book as guide in perfecting you photographic skills before, under and after a safari in Africa. I have assumed that you have a basic knowledge of photography. In this book I will cover topics for you to get a better understanding of photographic techniques such as lighting, composition, exposure and to get the most out of specific situations when photographing wildlife on safari in Africa.

In relations to camera equipment I will mention Canon as Canon is the brand that I use and have great experience with. I have no affiliations with Canon and you should be able to get similar equipment from other camera brands such as Nikon, or Sony/Minolta and other manufactures.

The accompanying website will enable you to keep learning as I post material on how you can improve your photographic skills, so take some time and visit: : **www.WorldOfSafari.com**

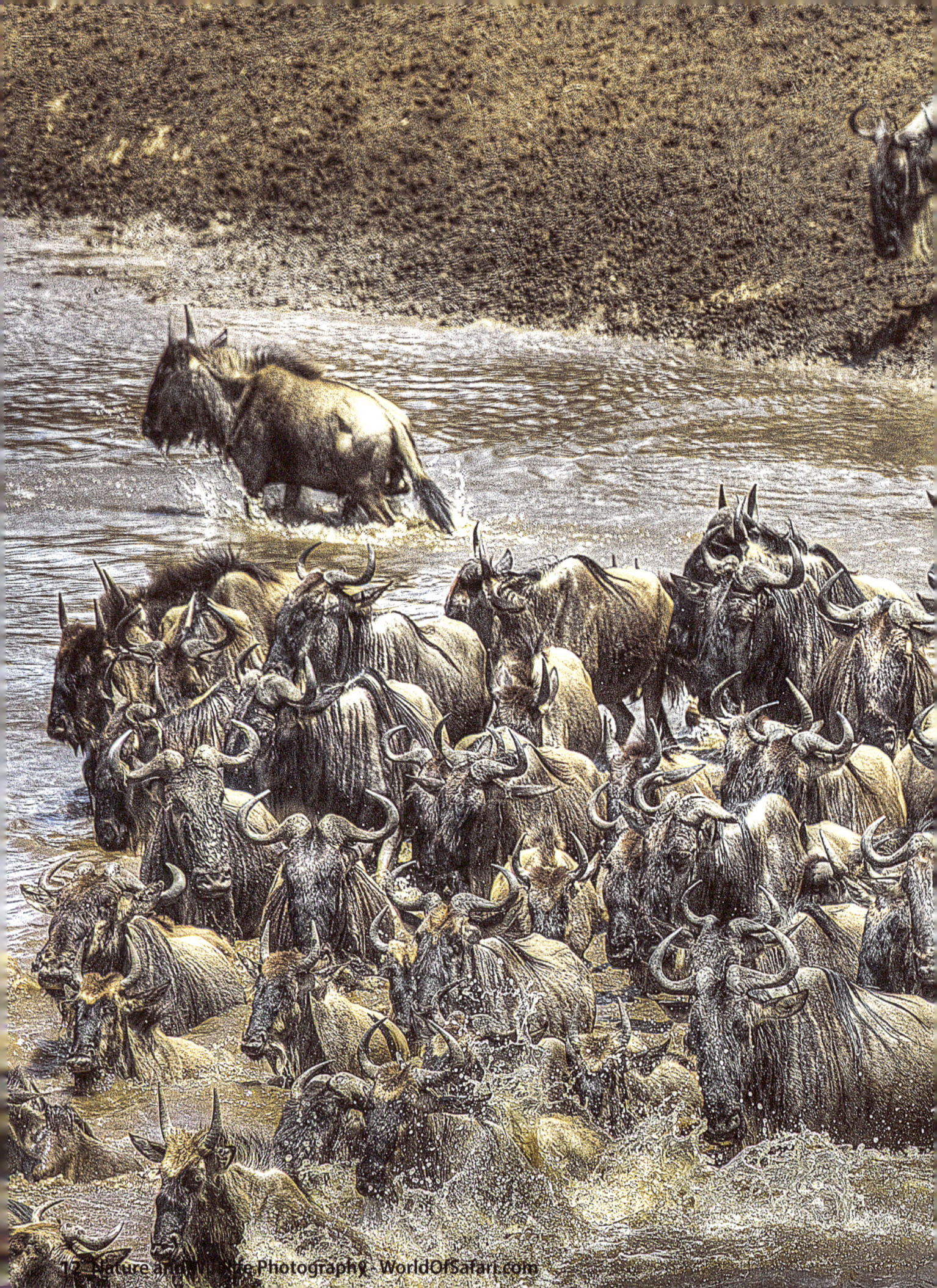

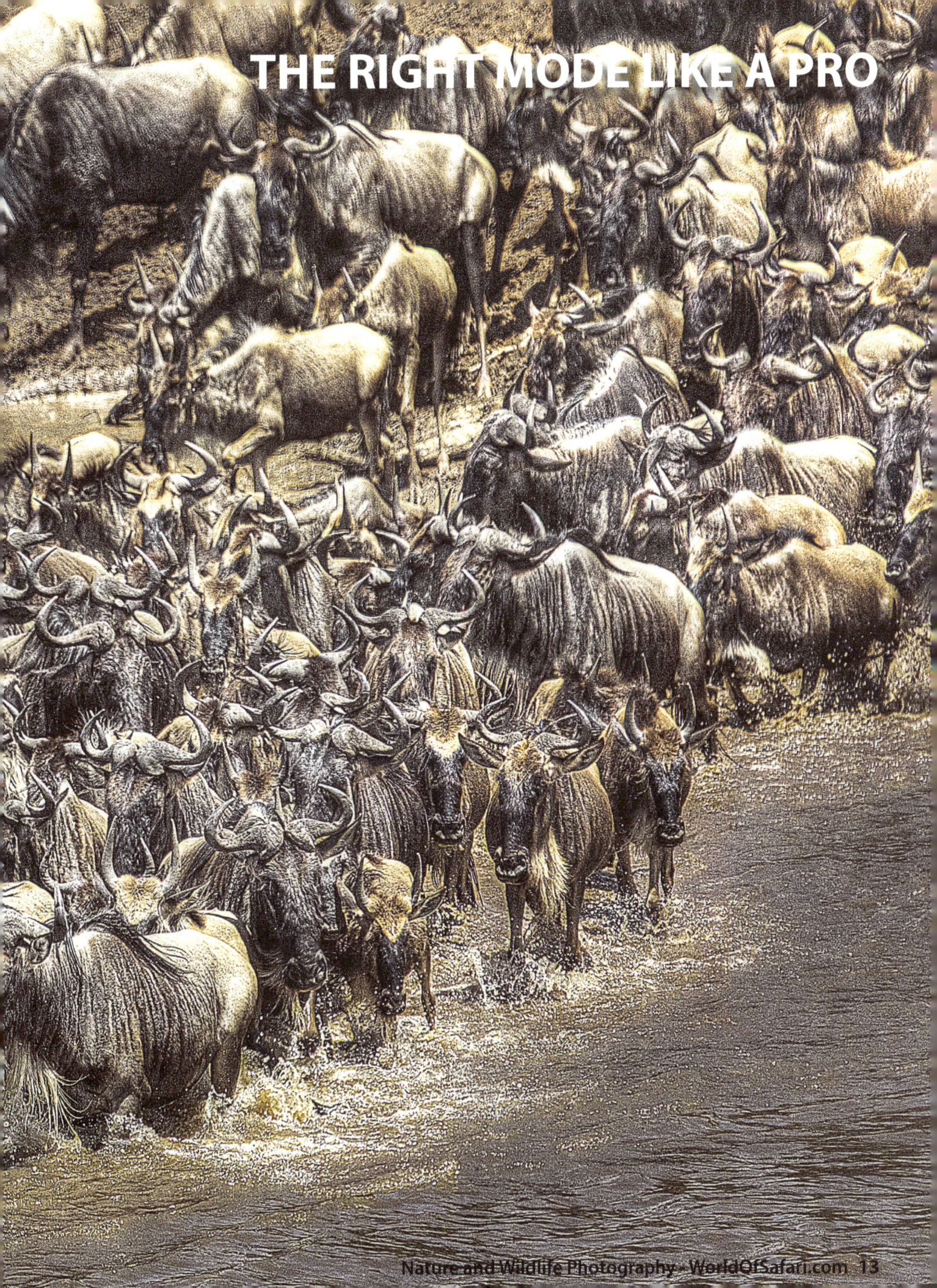

THE RIGHT MODE LIKE A PRO

Wildlife photography demands a blend of art and technology. You therefore need to learn how to get the right exposure for what you want to accomplish with your photograph. The exposure affects the colors and tones in a photograph which is why a good exposure is important to achieve.

Exposure is based on three variables:
- f-stop
- Shutter speed
- ISO

A good exposure gives you the tonalities and colors that make your photograph look its best for the light. The histogram is a valuable tool that can assist in creating a great exposed photograph which will be covered on page 53.

Camera bodies have several different exposure modes to choose from. It is always a good idea to become familiar with the different modes and know when to choose the best one for the photograph you are trying to capture. I always recommend reading your camera's manual and experience with the different modes to find the best choice for you for particular situations.

There are four creative exposure modes:
- Program
- Aperture Priority
- Shutter Priority
- Manual mode

Use the command dial on your camera to select the appropriate shooting mode. Consumer cameras include both basic modes and creative modes where the semi- and professional cameras only have the creative modes. I will not go into the basic modes but concentrate on how you can use the creative modes for the right situation.

In the creative modes, the camera can still offer some automatic function, but you have more control over the various aspects of capturing the photograph the way you see it.

Full Auto

Full Auto mode lets the camera control all the settings for you and all you have to worry about is point your camera at your subject and shoot away which leaves no control over the depth of field. Generally, you will want to have some control of either the shutter speed used to stop motion or the f-stop chosen to affect the depth of field.

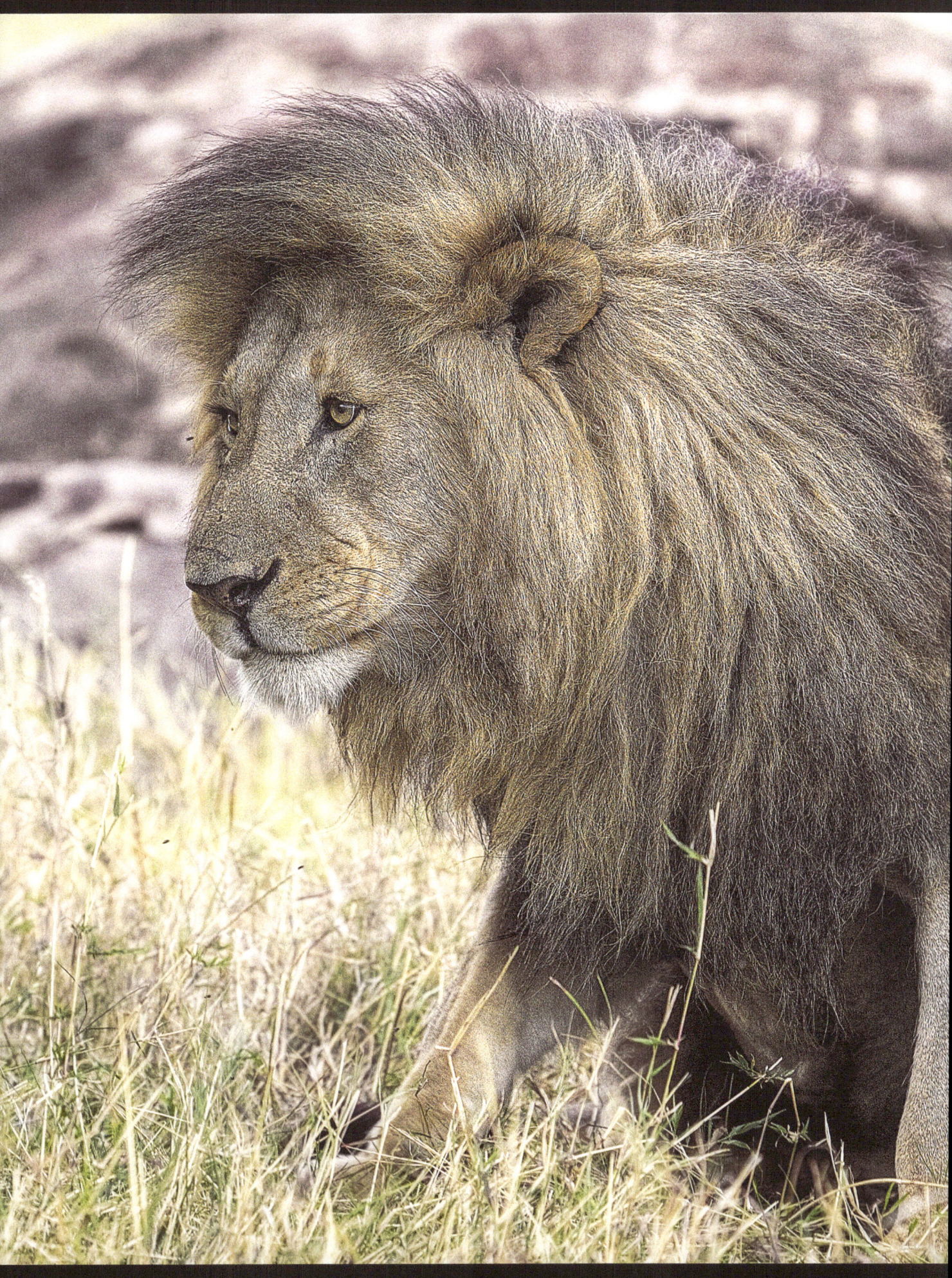

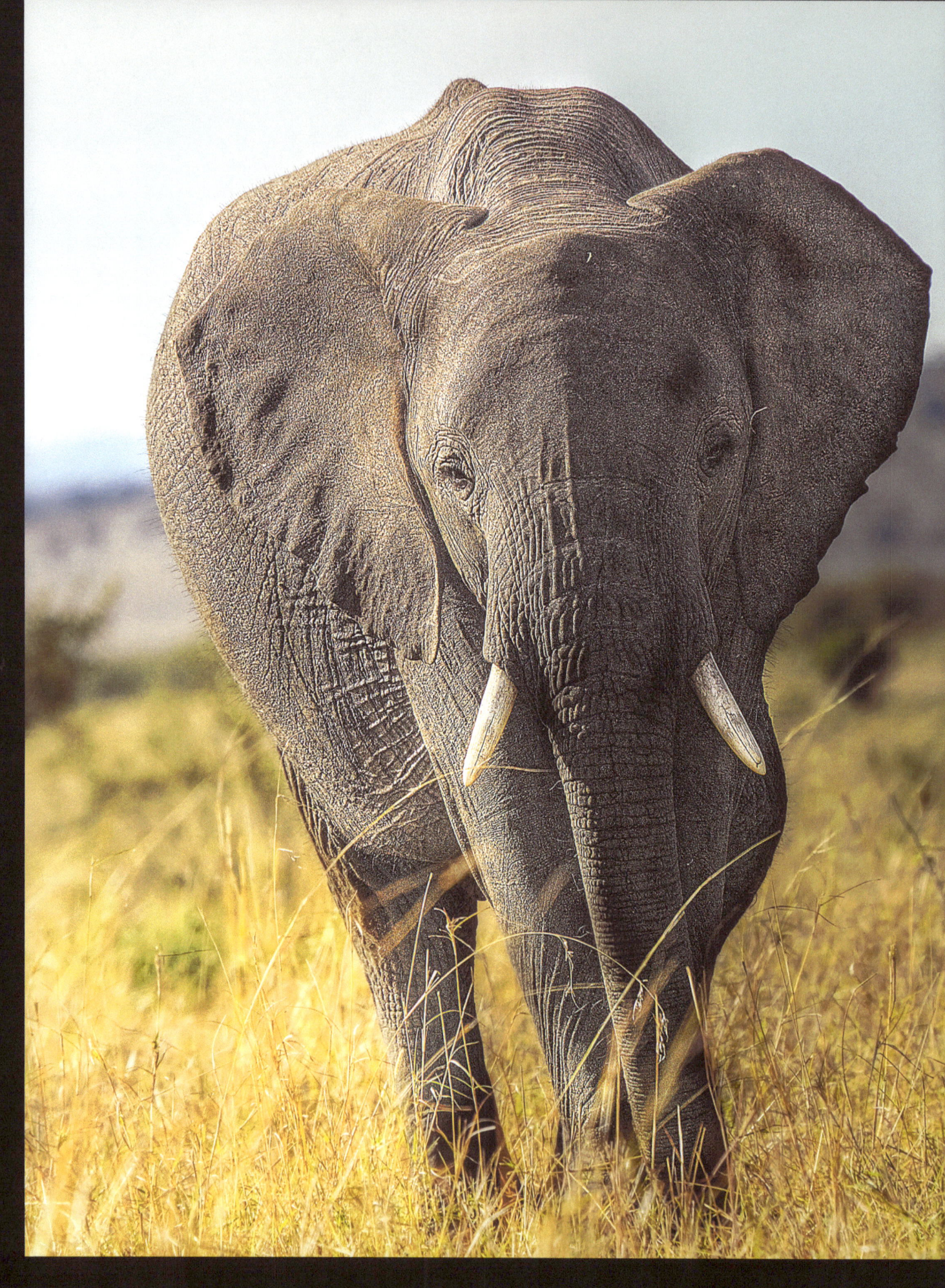

Program

Program mode (P) is a good beginner mode since it selects both the aperture (f-stop) and shutter speed at the same time. All you have to worry about is the ISO settings and the rest is done by the camera.

With program mode you pick different combination of shutter speed and aperture. If you do not like what the camera has chosen for you, it is easy to use the dial to change the setting of the combination. It is a better choice than full auto mode but still limited since you cannot set the exact shutter speed or f-stop you need for each photograph.

In Program mode you can change the Color Space and White Balance or just leave it as it is. Program mode is not very creative since you have little control of the end result. This mode is not my favorite choice since I like to have more control of my end results.

You can, however, adjust the exposure compensation to over- or underexpose your photo by -+3 stops by 1/3 increments. A stop is a measurement of exposure, measured in increments of exposure value also called EV. Exposure compensation will be covered later on page 61.

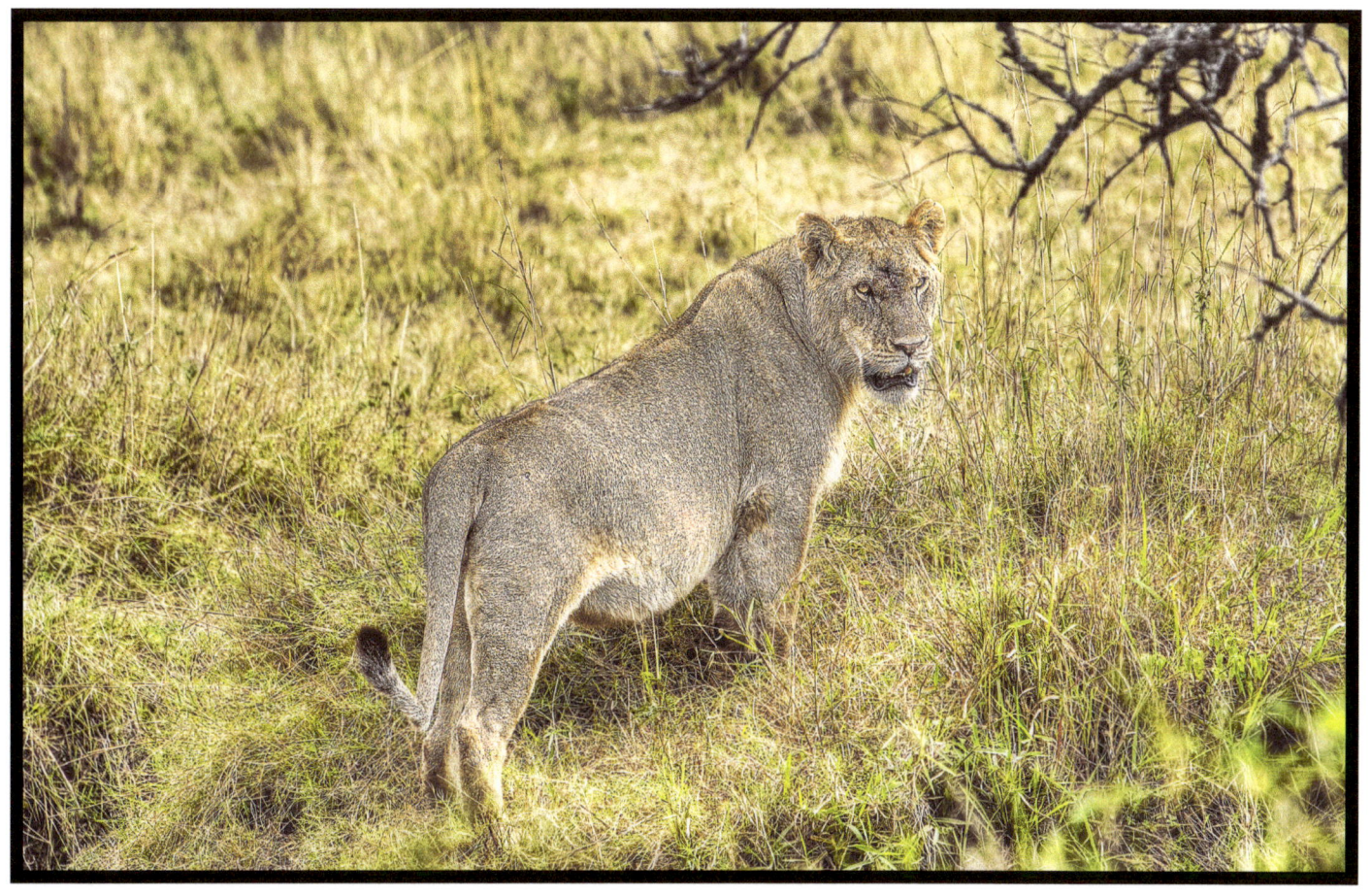

Aperture priority

Aperture priority mode (Av) enables you to select how large or small the aperture (f-stop) will be and therefore controlling the depth of field (how much the photograph should be sharp from front to back). When you choose the appropriate aperture, the camera automatically adjusts the shutter speed based on the lighting condition to match your choice of aperture (f-stop).

Each aperture (f-stop) step affects the amount of light reaching your camera sensor. For example, if you go from an aperture (f-stop) f2.8 to f5.6 you halve the light coming through the lens reaching your camera sensor. If you go from an aperture (f-stop) of f/4.0 to f/16.0 you go through four f-stops. On the other hand, if you go from an aperture (f-stop) of f/8.0 to f/4.0 you will double the amount of light reaching your camera sensor. You do not have to switch between full stops of light but can use halve and thirds stops. In addition to changing how much light is reaching your sensor, you are also affecting the depth of field and therefore how much the photograph is sharp from front to back.

Adjusting the aperture (f-stop) opens or closes a set of blades within your lens that controls the amount of light entering the camera to expose the photograph. The smaller the aperture number, the more open the aperture is and the more light can enter the camera which enables you to blur the background from your focusing point.

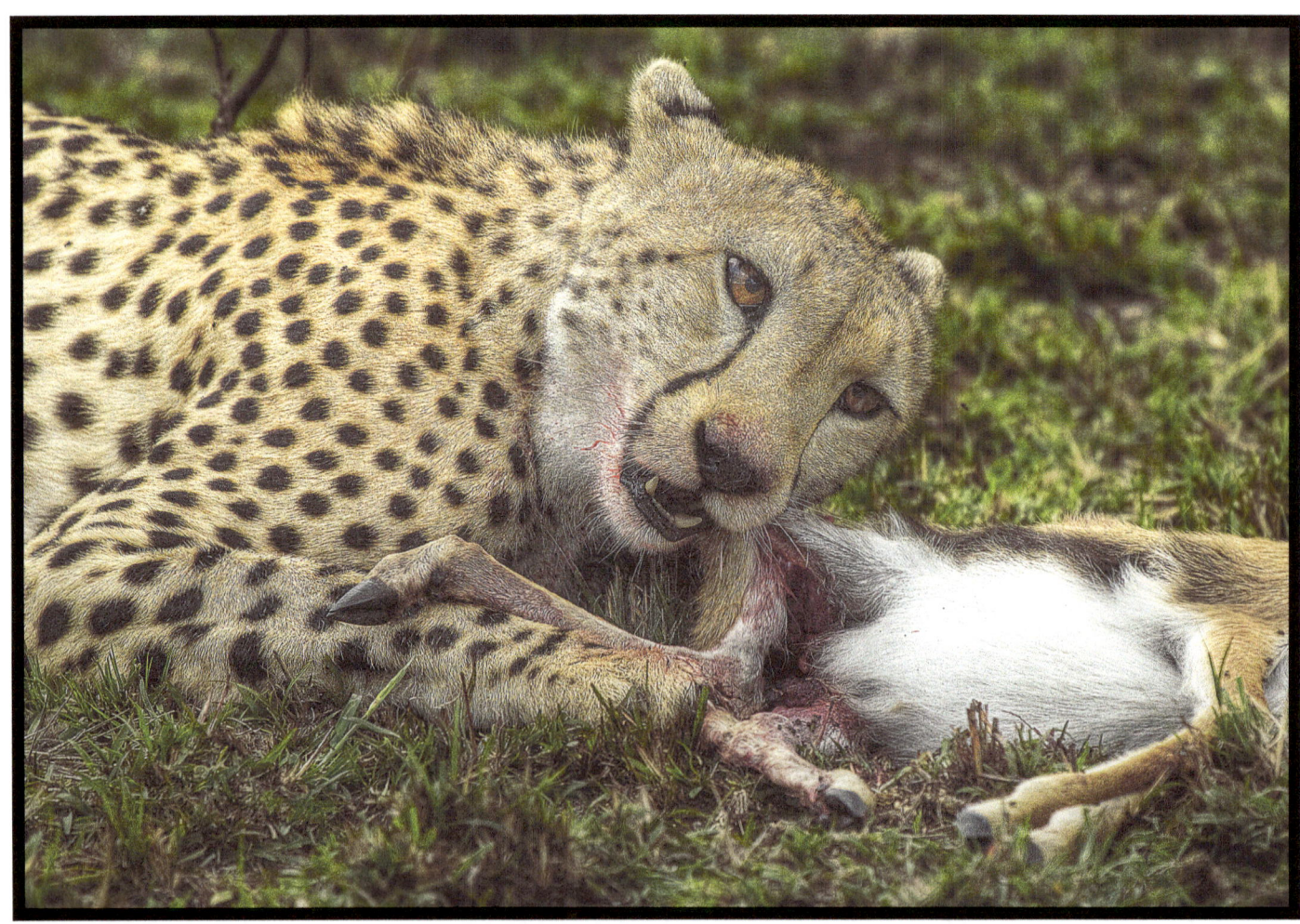

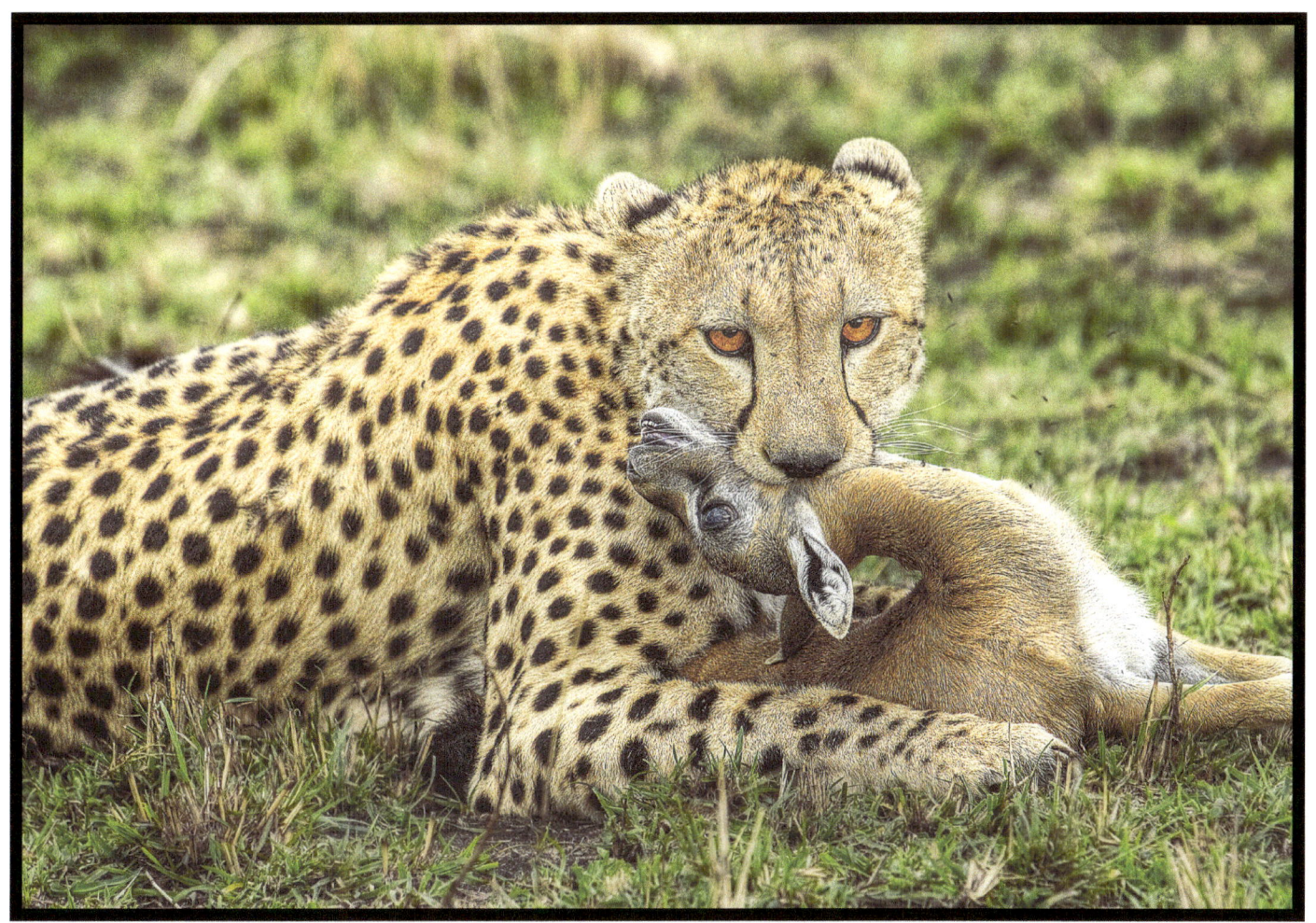

A large aperture number like f13 and above is used when you want the photograph to be sharp from front to back as for instance when photographing a landscape.

In aperture priority mode you control the depth of field and the camera then chooses the shutter speed for you to automatically get a good exposure. Aperture priority mode is the mode that I use the most for wildlife portrait photography since it enables me to choose the depth of field that I like for a particular animal or the situation at hand.

After photographing wildlife or landscape, I set my camera back to my default settings which is aperture priority mode with the largest possible aperture set ready for any action coming my way. The camera will then automatically choose the fastest possible shutter speed which enables me to freeze the action. I do take notice of the shutter speed and therefore adjust the ISO value accordingly to ensure that the shutter speed is fast enough for action.

If you always want the fastest shutter speed possible for any given situation, you can set the aperture to the lowest number and the camera will automatically adjust the shutter speed to the fastest possible based on the ISO speed your camera has been set to.

Shutter priority

Shutter priority mode (Tv) let you choose the shutter speed and the camera automatically selects the correct aperture (f-stop). By choosing shutter priority mode, you can choose to use a fast shutter speed to freeze motion when photographing animals or people, or you can use a long shutter speed to get motion blur to show motion.

The shutter speed is probably the easiest setting to understand as it simply means how fast the shutter opens and closes when you press the button. The faster the shutter speed, the easier it is to freeze movement and get a pin sharp photograph. The shutter speed is represented in seconds, a fast shutter speed would be 1/500th of a second, a slow shutter speed would be something like 1/60th of a second and a really fast shutter speed would be 1/1000th of a second. A long or slow shutter speed of 1/60th of a second and below can result in a blurry photograph which from time to time can create some interesting and creative effects to your photographs if done on purpose. The shutter speed also affects how much light is reaching your camera sensor. So while a fast shutter speed lets you freeze movements, it also requires more light, which is why you need to either use a larger f-stop such as f2.8, f4.0 or f5.6 or a higher ISO setting to get a correctly exposed photograph.

In some cases you do want to use a slow or very slow shutter speed to blur motion such as when photographing a waterfall or you want to blur the movement of a running animal.

If you are using a shutter speed shorter than the focal length of your lens, you should support your camera to minimize camera shake.

What you need to look out for, is that you do not underexpose your photograph due to a too fast shutter speed for a particular lighting condition.

The shutter priority mode is a good choice if you for instance want to blur a running subject. You can then set the shutter speed to 1/30 or of your choice. If you are panning the shot and want to get a blur trail from a running animal, ensure that you do not use a shutter speed faster than 1/125. On the other hand, if you want to freeze the action you need a faster shutter of 1/1000 and above depending on the animals speed.

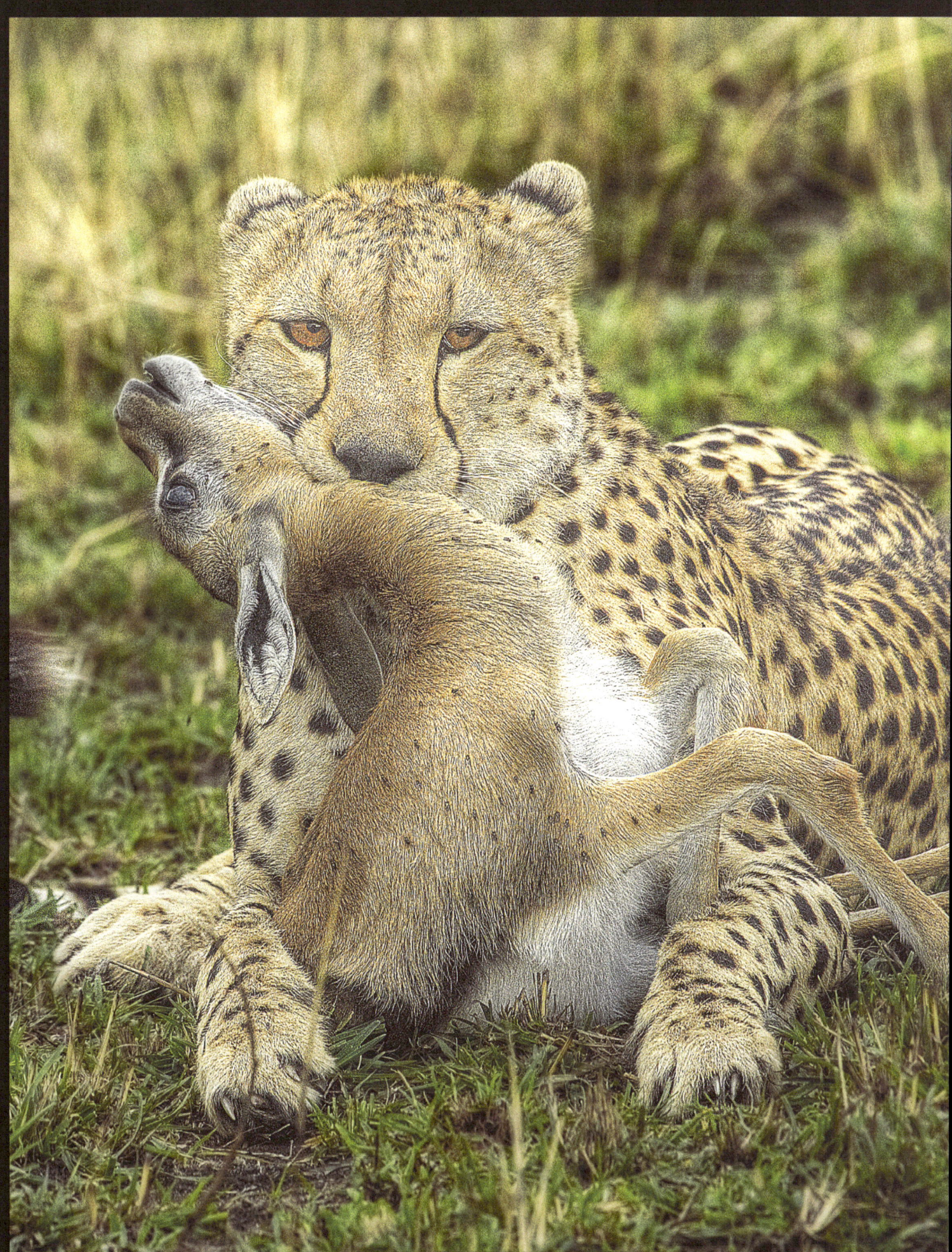

Manual

Manual mode (M) gives you complete creative freedom choosing both the aperture (f-stop) and the shutter speed. The important thing about manual mode is that you need to ensure your exposure is correct, so that you do not under- or overexpose your photograph. The manual mode gives you more control for situations where you have an animal moving fast in front of changing backgrounds such as light or dark backgrounds that definitely will confuse your camera's exposure reading.

The reason to learn manual mode is not to use it all the time, but give you the foundation to know how to use it from time to time when the other modes are not going to give you the creative results you are looking for. No matter how good the camera is, it does not know what you want to accomplish. You should take time to experience with manual mode and take full control over your photograph.

Some photographers use manual mode all the time, where I prefer to primarily use aperture priority mode and the switch to the other modes as needed. Manual mode is usually my last choice since I rarely have the time in the field to change all settings at the same time for photographing wildlife.

Find the right mode that works for you for specific situations which are why I encourage you to experiment with all the different modes until you get into the flow. Use manual mode if you take some photos of landscape or slow moving animals where you have plenty of time to set your settings. First of all, it will slow you down to focus more on composition, light direction and other aspects of taken the photograph, and secondly, it will enable you to experiment more allowing you to take several photos with minor adjustments.

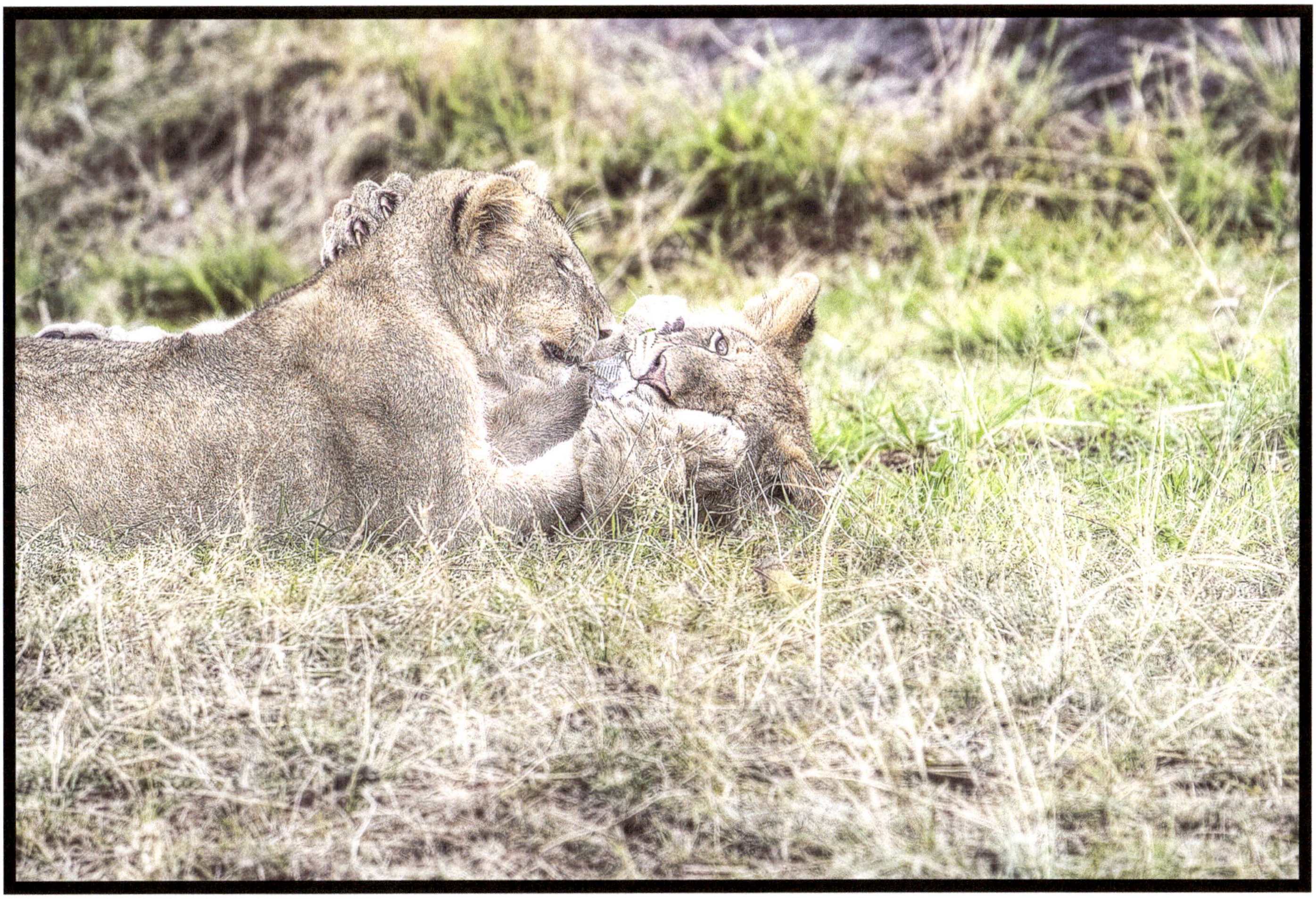

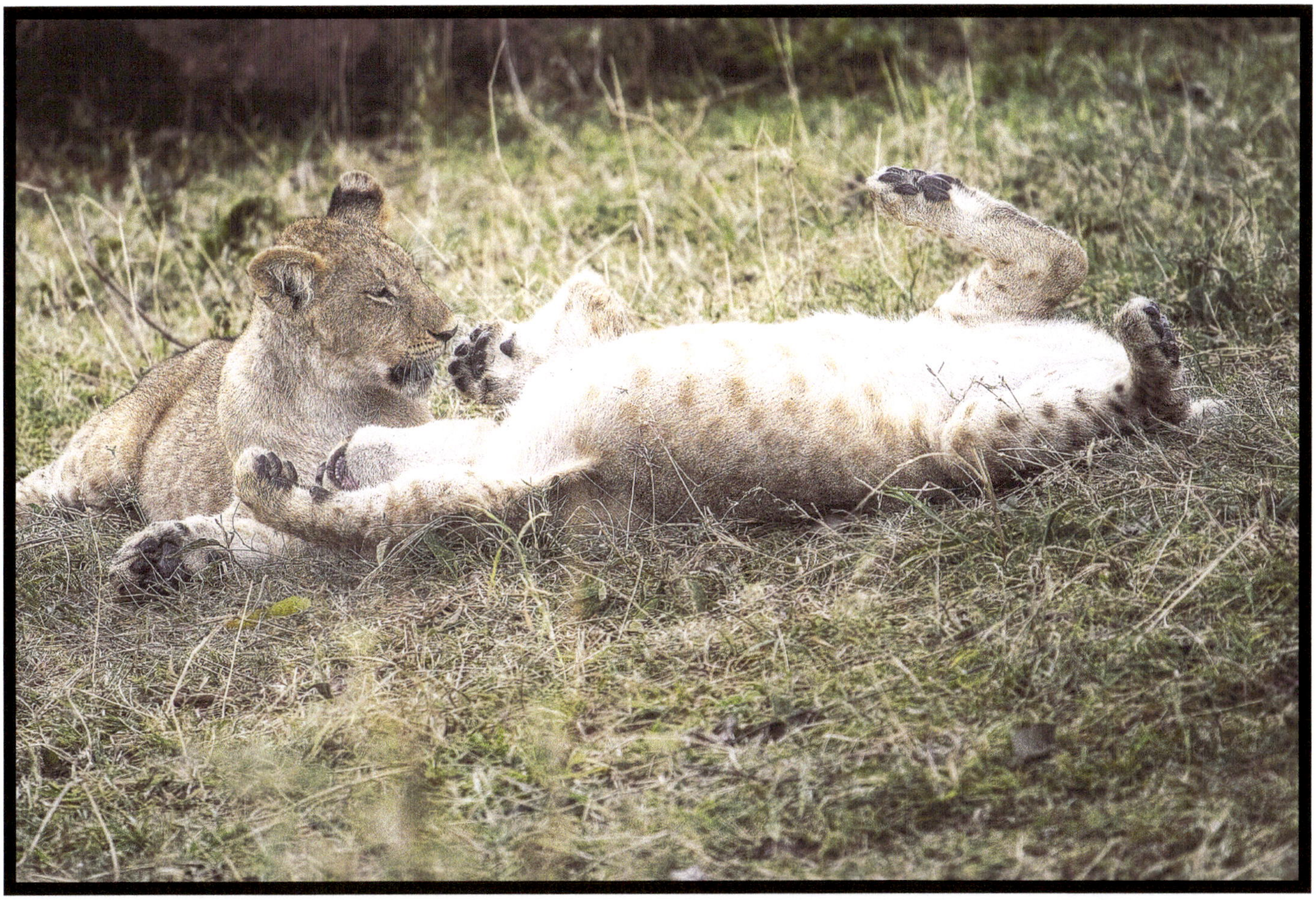

Nature and Wildlife Photography - WorldOfSafari.com

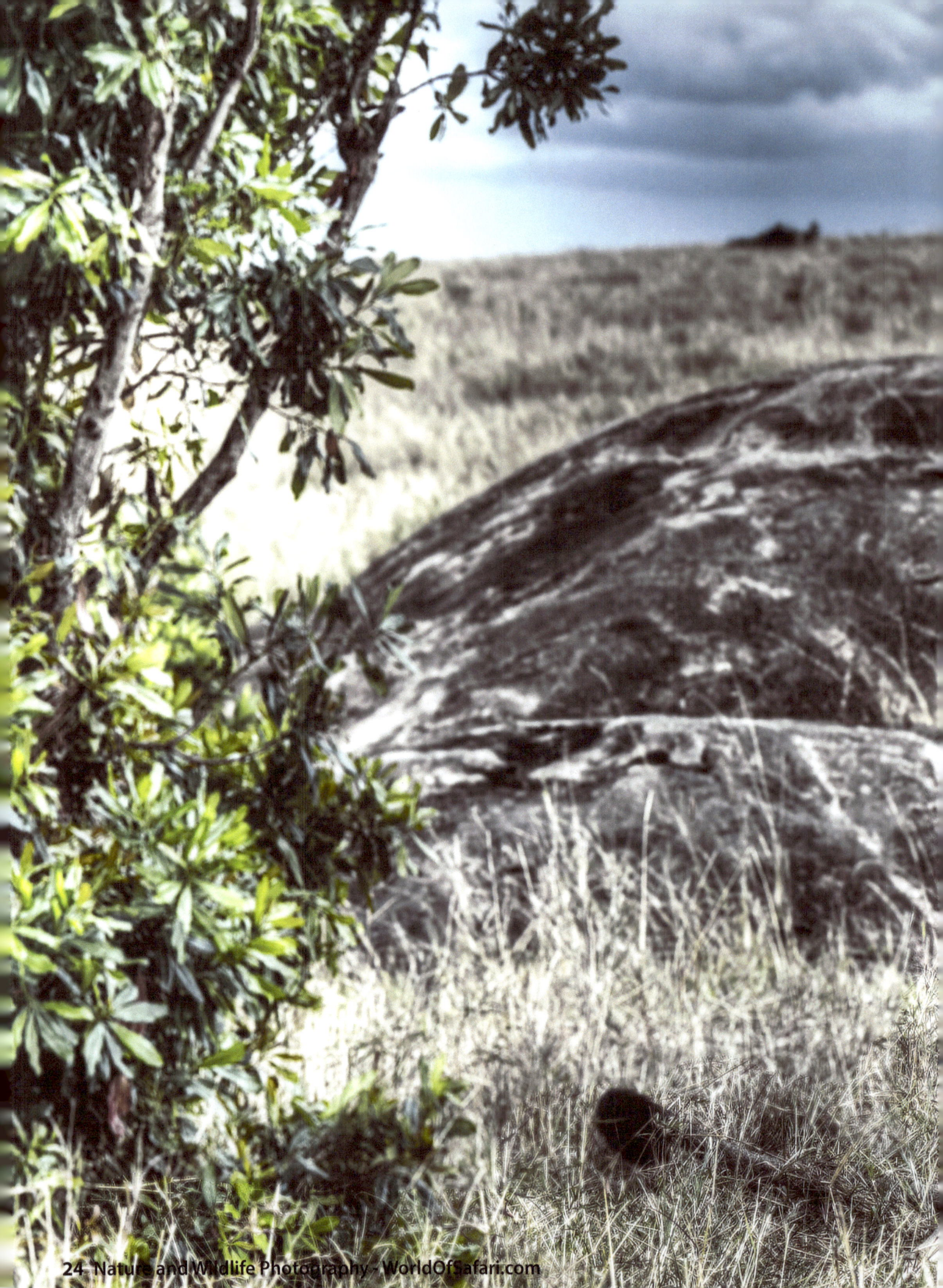

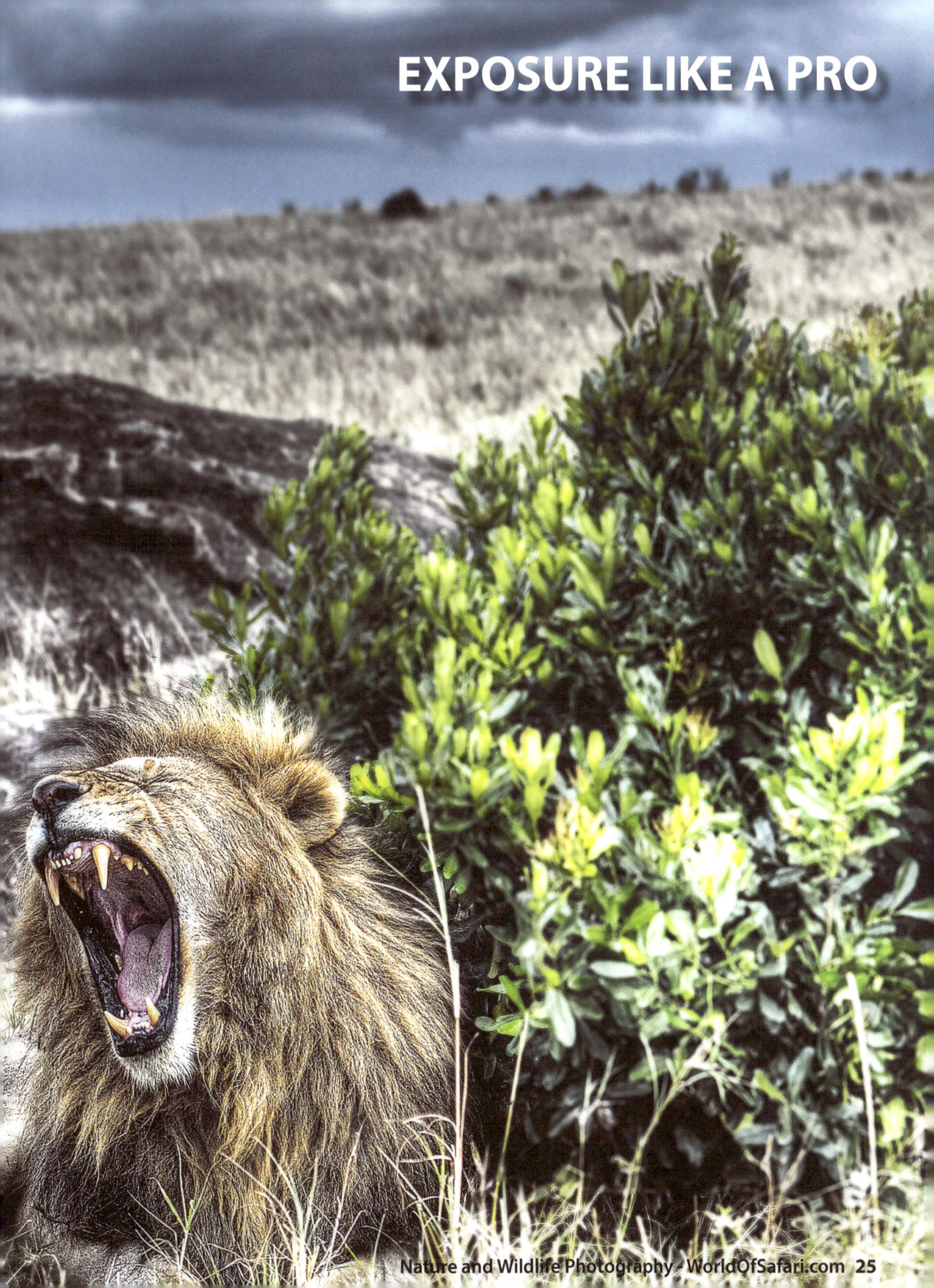

EXPOSURE LIKE A PRO

EXPOSURE LIKE A PRO

Exposure is the term used to describe the amount of light that is being recorded by your camera sensor. The exposure determines how bright or dark the photo will appear when it is captured. The key is to learn to read the tonality of the scene so that you can capture the effect you want in your photograph. On sunny days the range of tones between the highlights and the shadows are too great for the dynamic range of your camera sensor.

If too little light has not been recorded by your camera sensor your photo will be underexposed and appear too dark. If too much light has been recorded on the other hand your photo will be overexposed and appear too bright.

The lens aperture (f-stop) and shutter speed govern how much light reaches your camera sensor and by getting the combination right you will achieve a perfectly exposed photo. A perfectly exposed photo captures detail in both bright and dark areas of the photo. In an overexposed photo the brighter areas loose detail and are blown out. In an underexposed photo the shadows loose detail because they are too dark.

There are several exposure combinations that will result in a correctly exposed photograph. The combination of aperture, shutter speed and ISO setting you choose, must be related to the story you want to tell in your photo. Based on your creativity, you decide if the photo should be a pin sharp storytelling photo with great depth of field where everything is in focus, or a subject that pops against a blurry background.

The answer to obtain a good exposure is a compromise between choosing to expose your photograph for the highlights or for the shadows. Usually, it is better to expose for the highlights and loose details in the shadows since an overexposed photograph with a lot of blown highlights are less acceptable.

Wildlife scenes usually have areas of highlight that are not necessarily apparent and can spoil your photograph if they are blown out.

If your exposure appears as you have visualized it, then your exposure is correct. Exposure is not a mechanical thing that needs to be corrected every single time. It can be used in a creative way to self-express your own style of photography.

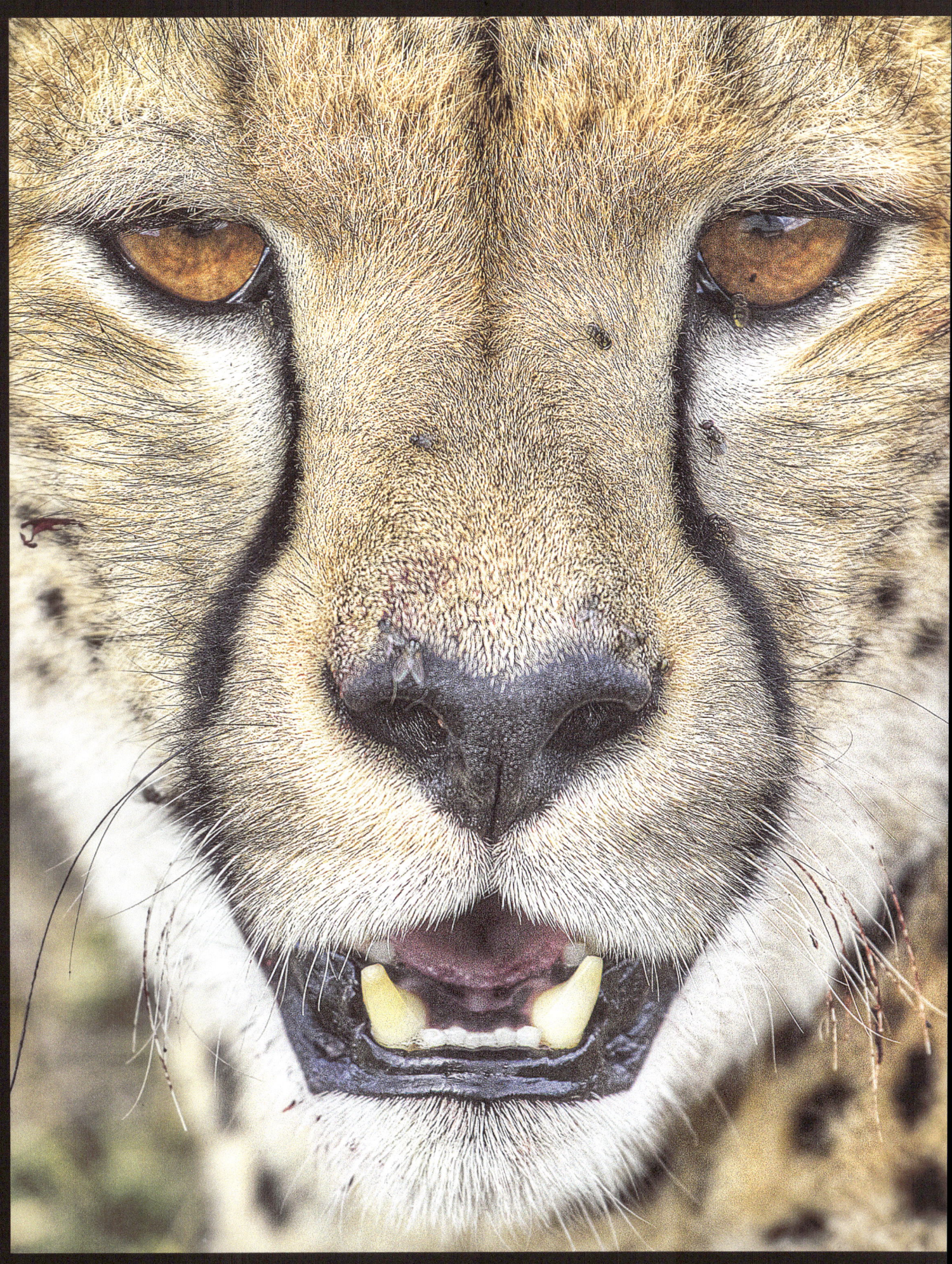

ISO

The ISO settings are equivalent to ISO used on film camera years back. It describes the camera sensor sensitivity to light. The lower the ISO setting the brighter the light is needed to make a correct exposure. The higher the ISO setting, the more light your camera sensor can pick up, but with a high ISO setting comes more noise in your photo. By changing the ISO settings from 100 to 200 enables you to photograph with twice the shutter speed at the same aperture.

As an example, if you set your camera at an aperture of f5.6, the ISO setting to 100, and the shutter speed of 1/125, then by changing the ISO setting to 200 you will get a shutter speed of 1/250 still with the same aperture of f5.6.

The lower the ISO setting you can use, the better your photograph quality will be. Most nature and wildlife photographers try to use as low and ISO setting as possible for the best photographic quality.

From time to time you do need to change the ISO speed to a higher setting than ISO 100 to get a fast enough shutter speed based on the lighting conditions which you work under. Do not be afraid to use a higher ISO speed as needed, just be aware of what it does to your photograph which is different from camera to camera.

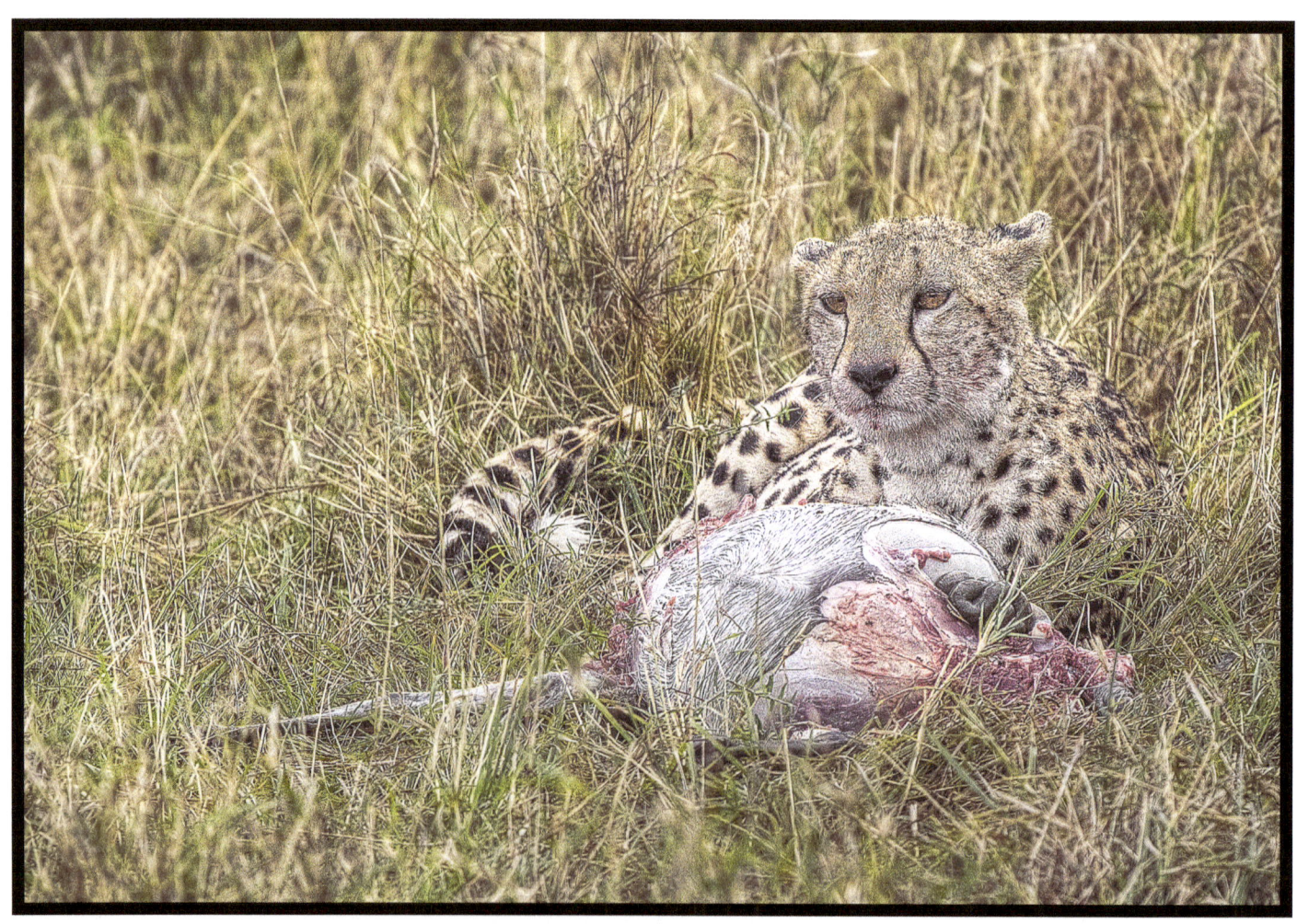

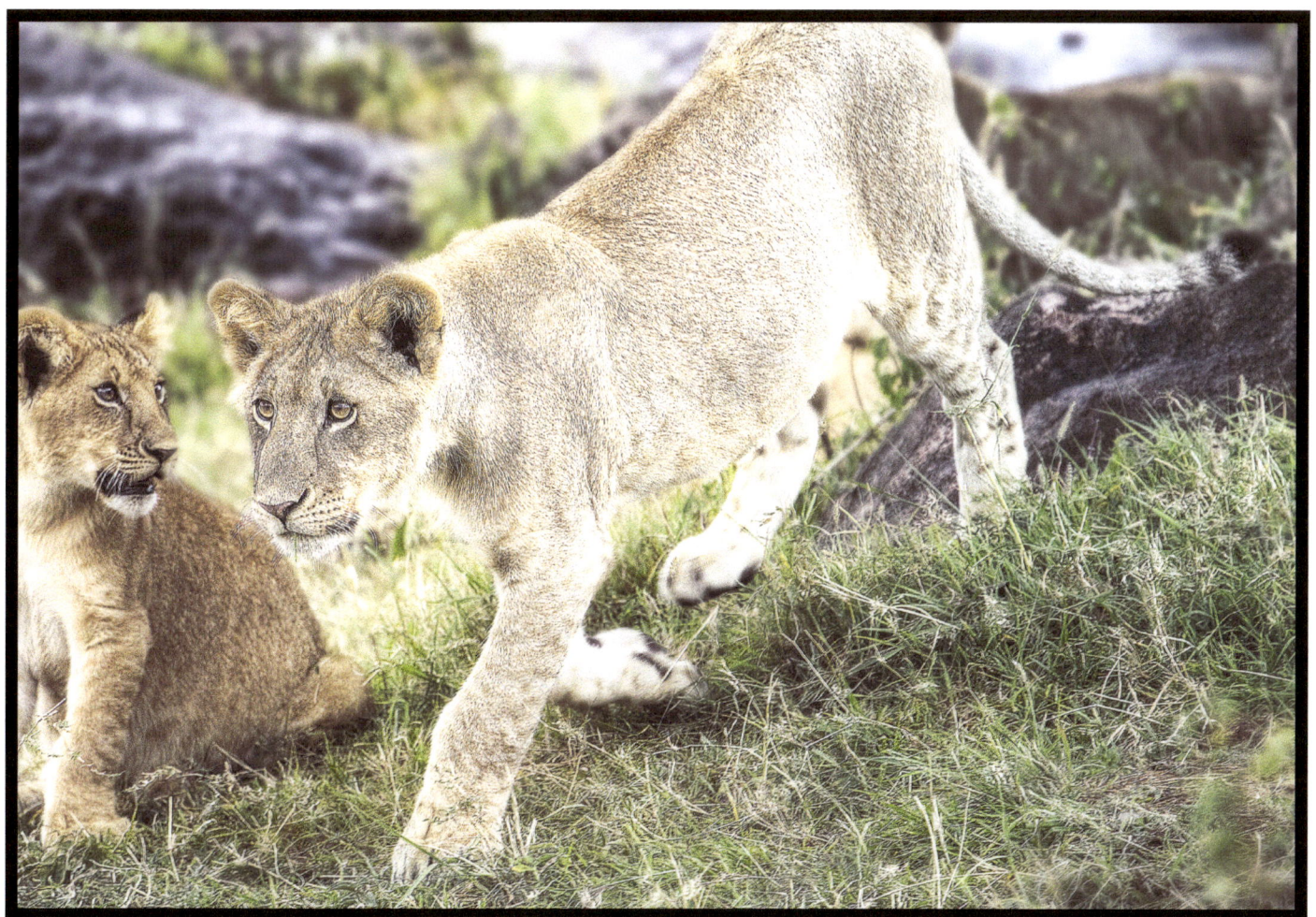

It is important to practice taking the same photo with different ISO settings with your camera to compare the result. You need to find out which ISO setting is the highest one you will allow yourself to use for a specific situation, since you will have to take into consideration the amount of noise which is going to be added by increasing the ISO setting to a higher number.

The more professional cameras have less noise at the same ISO settings than a cheaper consumer camera. Some consumer cameras cannot increase their ISO setting to more than 400 for acceptable results where a professional camera can increase the ISO setting to 1600 getting a similar result. The more expensive cameras work better under low light conditions than consumer cameras when it comes to noise.

Metering light

Digital cameras today have a very effective metering system especially for front-lighting, but do not expect your camera to get it right every time.

However, high contrast scenes like scenes with direct sunlight and shade have more contrast than your camera sensor can record and your camera metering system will therefore expose for only some parts of the scene and leave some parts of the scene too dark or too bright.

On a sunny day colors will look less saturated since sunlight will obscure the colors on anything that reflect light such as leaves and flowers.

The golden hour at dawn and dusk where the sun is rising or setting can be tremendously helpful since your camera sensor is able to record most of the light in the scene. When the sun is low in the sky, the sun casts long and soft shadows and the color of the light is often more warm and pleasant. With the sun at a lower angle, there is less contrast and therefore your camera sensor will be able to record most of the scene's tonal range. The long and soft shadows during the golden hour are more pleasing in a photograph than the harsh shadows created during mid-day.

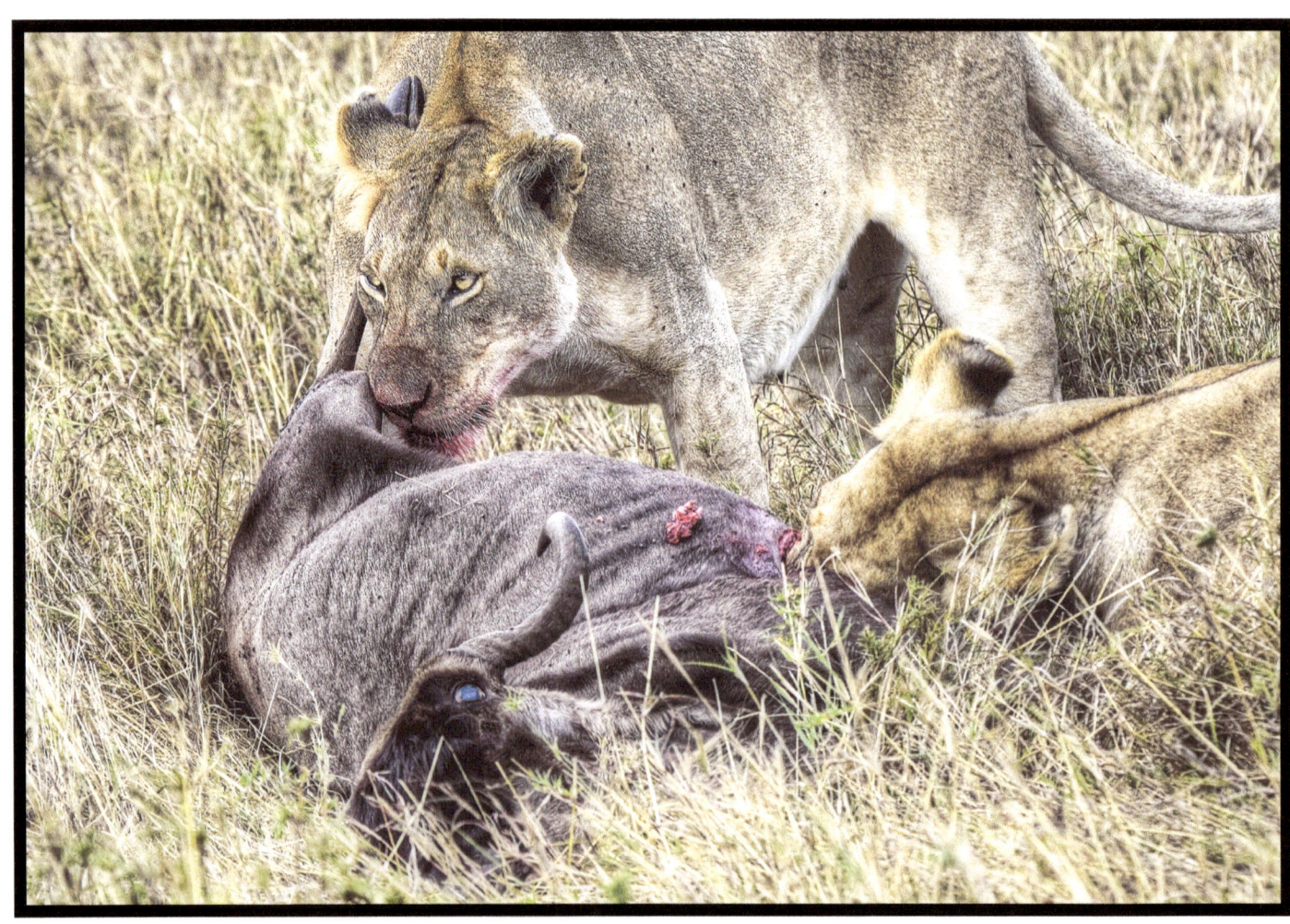

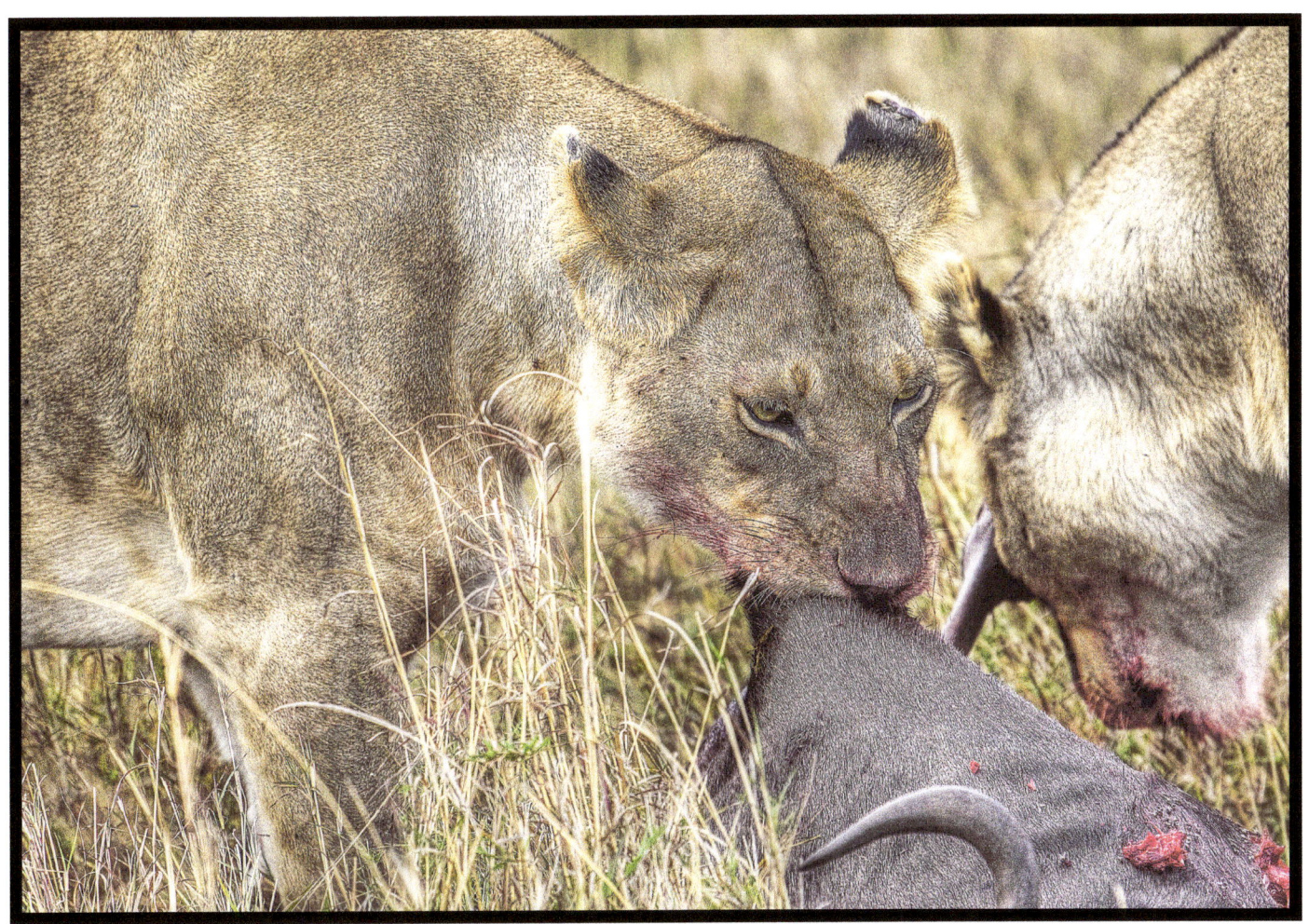

If you have time for it in the wild, try to get a spot reading of something that has a similar color scale as a gray card (middle tone colors) for a more precise reading.

Another way is to bracket your photo for the best selection in the dark room afterwards.

Your camera takes a light metering from all over the scene (depending on the metering mode) and calculate what it believes will give you a perfect exposure. No matter how good these calculations are they cannot give the results you want every time.

At dusk these two lionesses were feeding on a wildebeest they had just killed. I used evaluated metering mode to ensure that I got a tonal reading of the whole scene as the lionesses were blending in with the high grass. For the photograph of the lionesses with their kill I used an aperture f/9.0 at ISO 400 with a shutter speed of 1/125 (Bottom left).

In another photograph of the two lionesses with their kill, I used an aperture f/8.0 at ISO 800 with a shutter speed of 1/250. There were not much light to work with and I was not too happy with the low shutter speed, but the alternative would have been less depth of field or an higher ISO setting which I was trying not to use (Top).

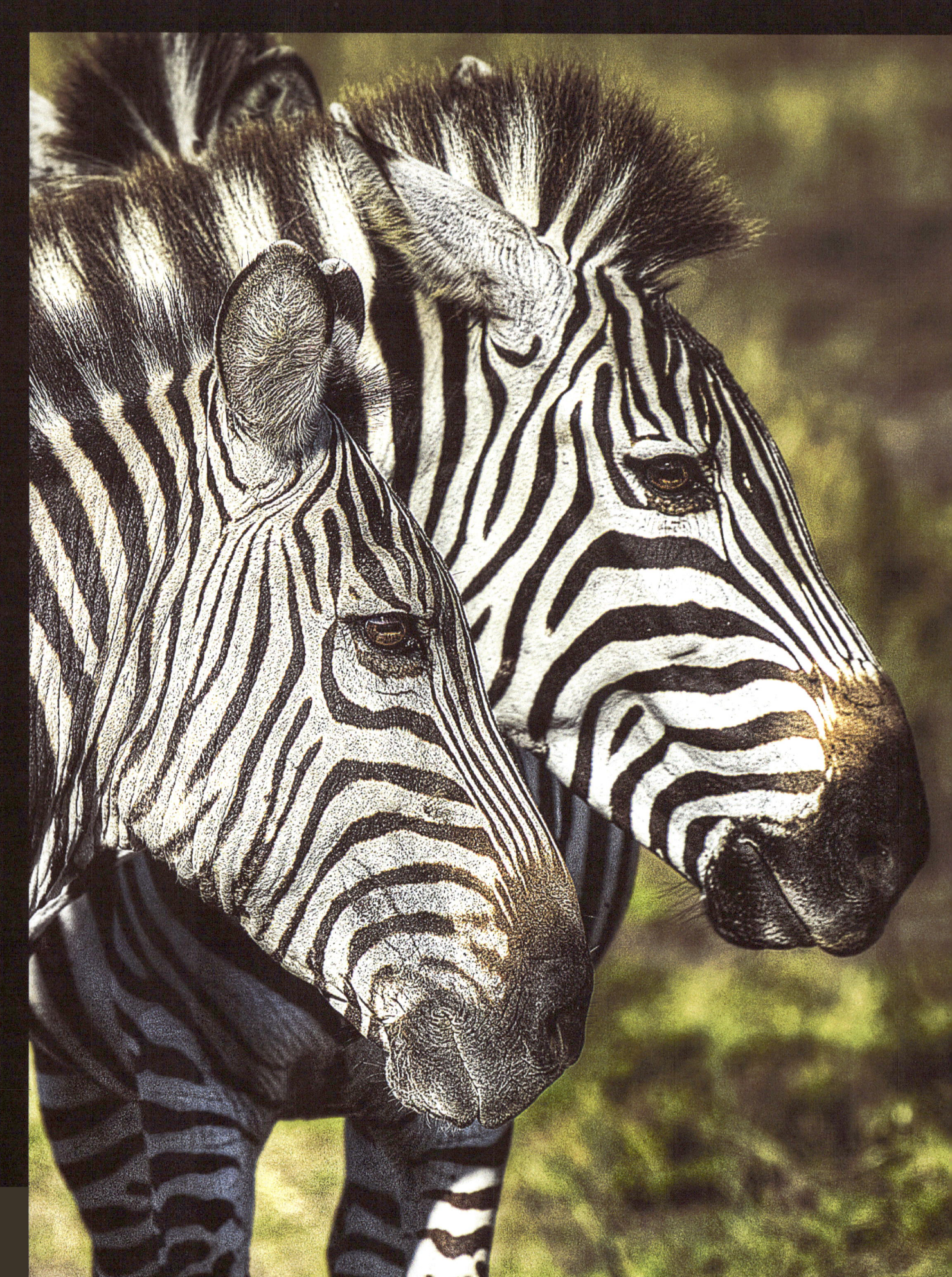

Exposure compensation

There are situations where we know for a fact that the camera metering system will always get it wrong and that is with very dark or white animals. Very dark animals like rhinos, elephants and buffalo are hard for your camera to meter. Therefore, make sure to dial in -1 or more to compensate for the camera's overexposed reading.

If the animal is completely white, you should in most cases use an exposure compensation of +2, and if it is completely black you should use -2 in exposure compensation. Having said that, it is always a compromise where you try to expose your photo including both the animal and the environment and at the same time having a large scale of tonality to deal with.

You should remember that underexposed photos are recoverable compared to an overexposed photo where the highlights have been blown out.

If your scene includes a wide range of tones, you will have to decide on which element are the most important for you to expose correctly. So basically, when photographing a wild animal in its environment you need to decide if you expose for the animal or for the surroundings. My choice would be on the animal since the habitat the animal lives in is secondary to me.

It is important to remember that after you have been photographing using exposure compensation that you set it back to zero, so that you do not accidently under- or overexpose the next photo.

Exposure compensation affects both color and tone. Overexposure tends to wash out colors while underexposure saturates the colors. This is something you should be aware of when using exposure compensation. Grass, for instance, can benefit from a little underexposure where flowers in general need a slight overexposure.

When photographing a light or dark scene with average tonal values either very dark or very light, your camera metering system will try to make the tonal values average of 18% grey. This means that a very dark scene will be overexposed which require exposure compensation to compensate for the metering done by your camera to get the results you want.

High contrast scenes have more light than your camera can record. With your eyes you can see 10 - 14 stops of light (depending on the brightness and contrast in the scene) and your camera (most) can record only 5 - 9 stops, which mean that your camera will not be able to record exactly what you see. High contrast scenes with direct sunlight and shades will have more contrast than your camera can record which is why you must choose which parts of the scene are important to you and ensure your exposure by your camera is recording those areas.

Exposure is an artistic vision of what you want and not what the camera calculates. Therefore, you must make a choice of dialing in exposure compensation to achieve the proper results in your photographs.

The exposure compensation can been seen in your viewfinder like this:

$$-2..1..0..1..+2$$

The marker will likely be at zero when you have not made any changes to your exposure compensation. As you turn your exposure compensation dial, you will see the marker moving to the left or right on the scale. Most cameras (besides the professional range) have exposure compensation from -2 to +2. If you move the scale to -1 your shutter speed will be shorter by 1 stop making your photo half as bright. If you move the marker to +2 you are slowing the shutter speed down by 2 stops making your photo 4 times as bright. You should refer to your camera's manual for setting the exposure compensation on your camera. I prefer using aperture priority mode when using exposure compensation.

The Masai giraffe was photographed as a scenic composition with the beautiful environment to be found in Masai Mara, Kenya. I used evaluative metering which I used most of the times with an aperture of f/10.0 at ISO 100. The photograph was captured late afternoon so I used an exposure compensation of -1 to dial in more detail in the sky. I used a shutter speed of 1/400 to ensure that there were no camera shake (Top right).

I also like to capture the aftermath of a kill even though there are so many animals to photograph in Masai Mara. When I came across this wildebeest caracas on the plains in the high grass, I used an exposure compensation of -2/3 to underexpose a little for the wildebeest's head or what was left of it. I used an ISO of 100 with a shutter speed of 1/200th of a second, and the aperture was set to f/11.0 for detail from front to back (Bottom right).

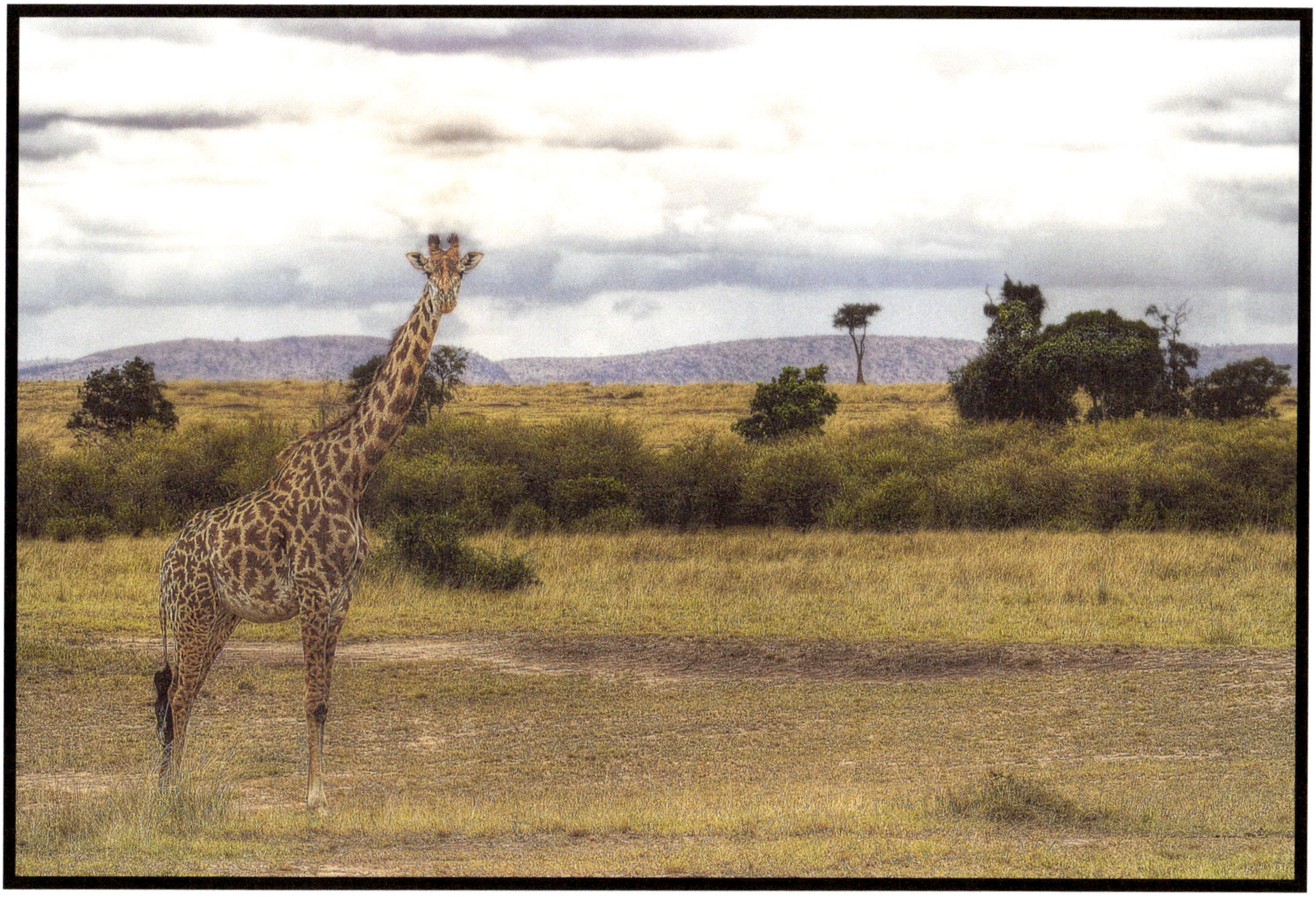

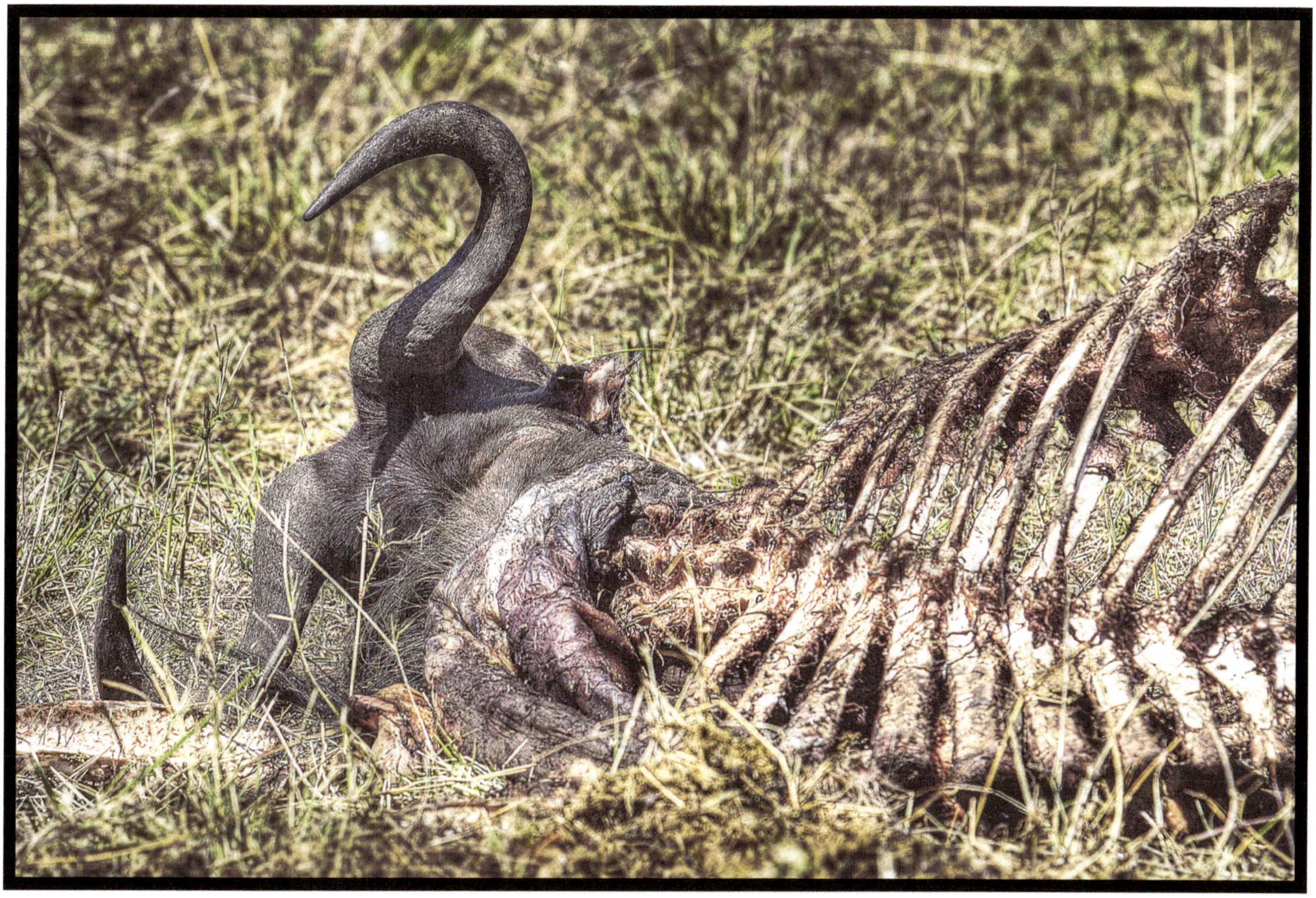

Nature and Wildlife Photography - WorldOfSafari.com 35

The sunny 16 rule

During the mid-day on a sunny day it can be difficult for your camera meter to get the exposure right. An old rule for estimating the exposure is the sunny 16 rule. By memorizing the sunny 16 rule you will always be able to set a correct exposure without any tools.

In bright sunlight you can use the sunny 16 rule by setting the aperture (f-stop) to f16 and the shutter speed to the inverse of the ISO. So, if your ISO are at 100 and the f-stop at f16, the shutter speed must be set to 1/100. You do not have to use f16 for this rule to work. If your ISO is set at 100 and you set your f-stop to f2.8, you must set your shutter speed at 1/3200.

For more info see the accompanying sunny 16 chart.

f-stop	ISO 50	ISO 100	ISO 200	ISO 400
f/2.8	1/1600	1/3200	1/6400	
f/4.0	1/800	1/1600	1/3200	1/6400
f/5.6	1/400	1/800	1/1600	1/3200
f/8.0	1/200	1/400	1/800	1/1600
f/11	1/100	1/200	1/400	1/800
f/16	1/50	1/100	1/200	1/400
f/22	1/25	1/50	1/100	1/200
f/32	1/12	1/25	1/50	1/100

Light meters get fooled when metering off very bright or dark subjects which is the reason why we need to use exposure compensation. Exposure compensation can also be hard to determine during mid-day when the light is very bright. Your camera is trying to meter for 18% gray using a reflected meter reading, but in the real world things are not always medium tones, especially during mid-day where everything becomes overly bright.

The sunny 16 rule is based on the fact that the light from the sun is equally bright during from 10 am to 5 pm plus/minus an hour or two depending on the time of year. Incidence lighting which the sunny 16 rule is based on does not depend on the subject, only the intensity of the lighting.

Do not rely exclusively on the rule - it is only a guideline for photographing animals under bright lighting conditions.

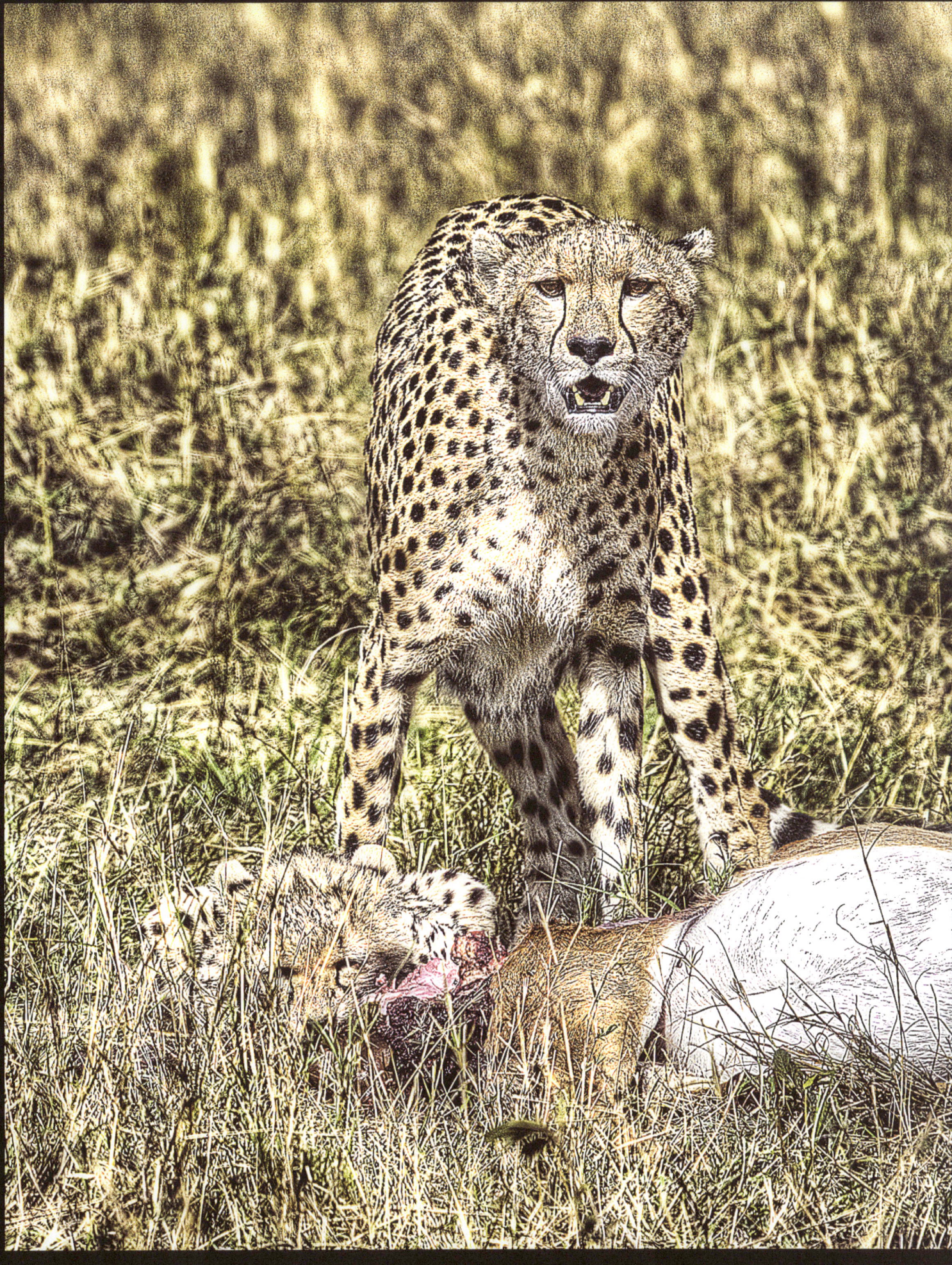

Bracketing

Exposure bracketing is the practice of taking several identical photos of a scene with different exposures to ensure that just one is properly exposed.

As an example you can take a meter reading of your subject and then take three photos:
- One slightly underexposed using exposure compensation of -1.
- One with no exposure compensation.
- One slightly overexposed using an exposure compensation of +1.

You do not need to use -/+ 1 in exposure compensation when bracketing, you can also try using smaller exposure values (EV) such as 1/3 or 1/5. Exposure Bracketing is most useful under difficult lighting conditions or if you are simply in doubt that your exposure setting is right.

I do recommend that you take several photos of the animals with different exposures, if you are unfamiliar with your metering. You can also set up your camera to use auto exposure bracketing (AEB) when you take your photo. Most cameras are as default set to take three photos in a row to compensate for over- or underexposed photos, you might be able to change it depending on the camera body (See your manual for how to change it if needed).

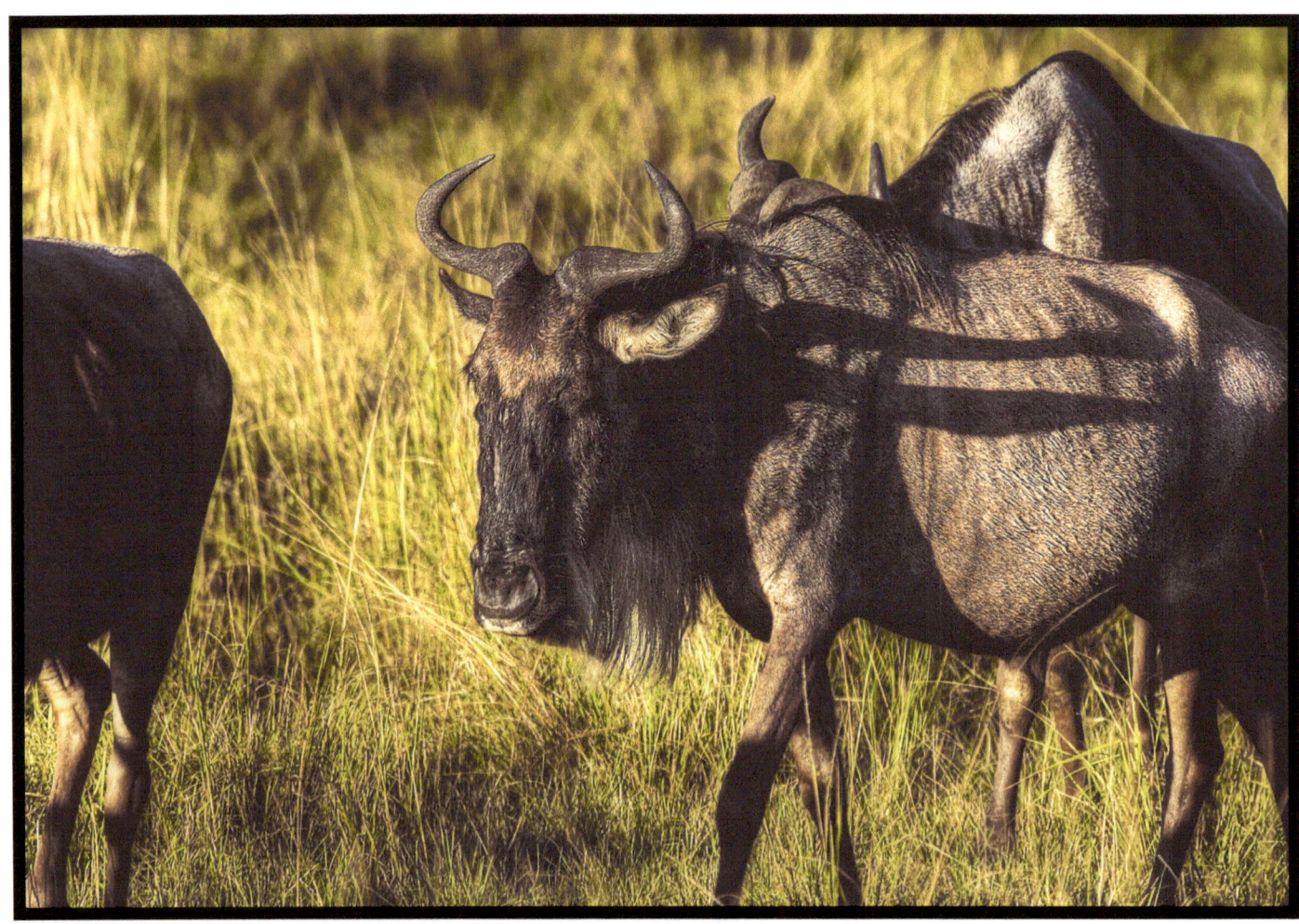

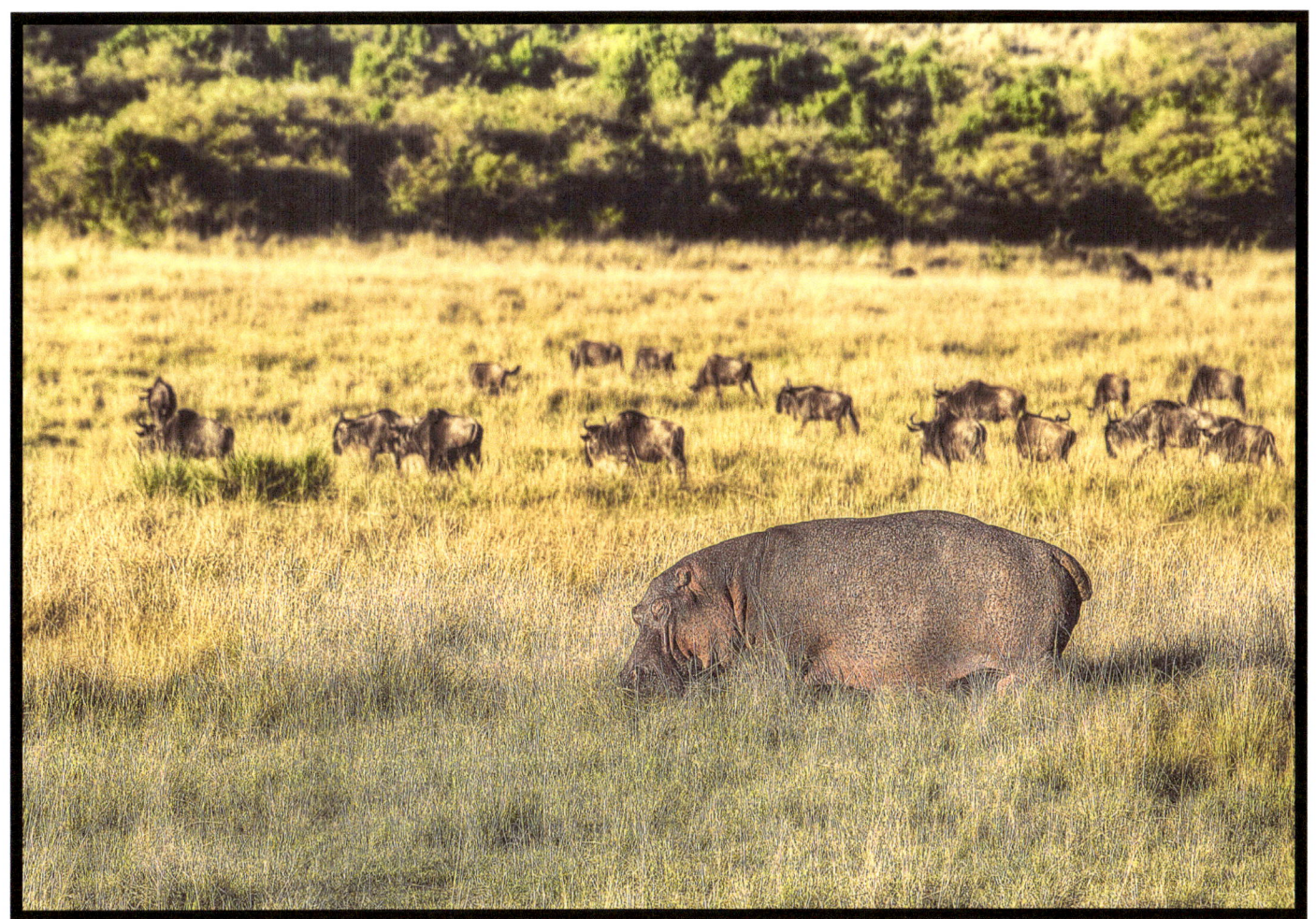

It is not really suitable to bracket your photos when photographing action. If you take your photos in RAW format, you will allways be able to change the exposure later in the dark room. I always take my photos in RAW format just in case I did not get the exposure right in the first place.

At dusk a hippo was grassing on the banks of the Mara River. The light was golden and I knew that the hippo comes in the category where you most likely need to use exposure compensation to get it right. The golden light did create a nice tonality on the hippo so I bracketed my photos to ensure getting the exposure right. I used an aperture f/9.0 at ISO 200 with a shutter speed of 1/250th of a second (Top).

A herd of wildebeest was also grassing next to the hippo in the same golden light at dusk. I used an aperture f/9.0 at ISO 200 with a shutter speed of 1/160th of a second. The photo of the wildebeest was also bracketed since they were moving slowly on the banks of the Mara River (Bottom left).

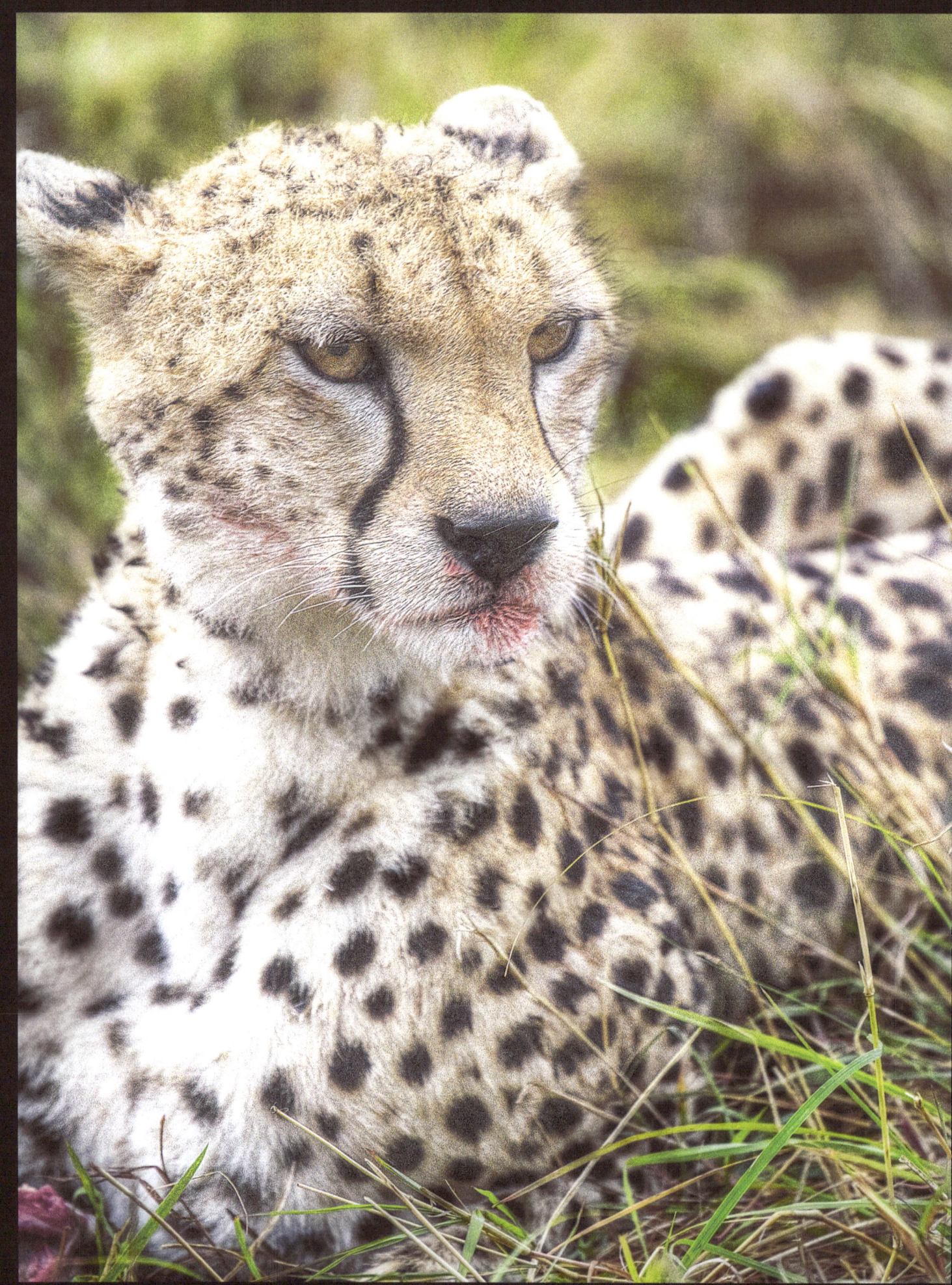

Histogram

The histogram is probably the least understood tool in your digital arsenal and one of the most important when it comes to perfecting the exposure of your photographs. The easiest way to learn how to properly expose your photographs is by learning how to use the histogram.

The histogram helps you see if your exposure is just right or if it is under- or overexposed. The histogram is a graph of tonalities that your camera sensor sees. When you look at the histogram, you see a graph of the light levels present in your photo and in most cases the graph looks like a simple bell curve meaning it is not over- or underexposed.

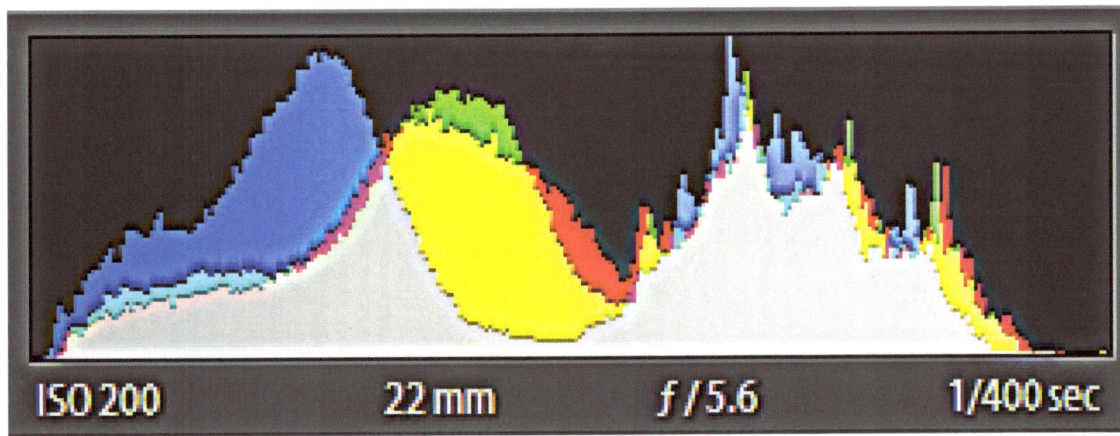

Figure above shows the bell curve centered meaning that the exposure is correct.

The left side of the histogram represents shadow and the amount of black in the photograph. The right side of the histogram represents highlights and the amount of white in the photograph. You can easily see if there is a problem with the exposure by the shape of the histogram graph and how the left and right sides interact.

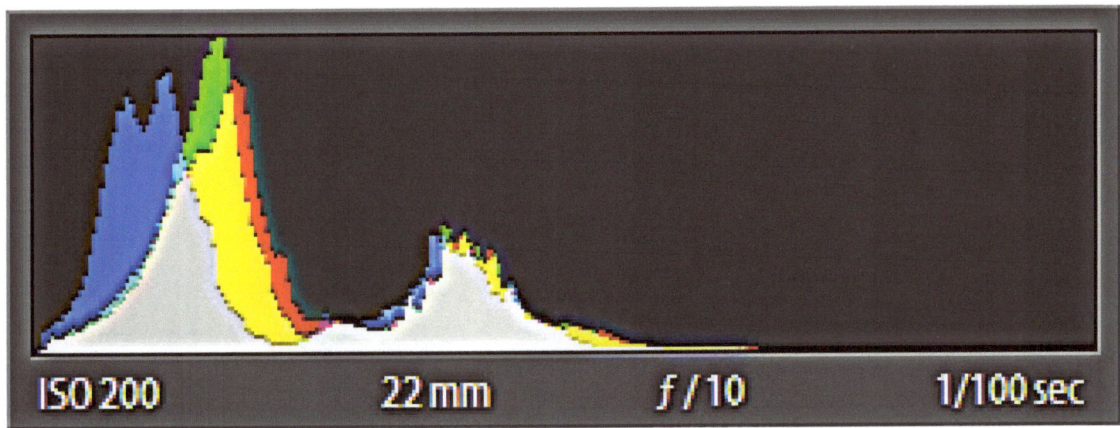

Figure above shows a histogram which is too far to the left, meaning the photo is underexposed.

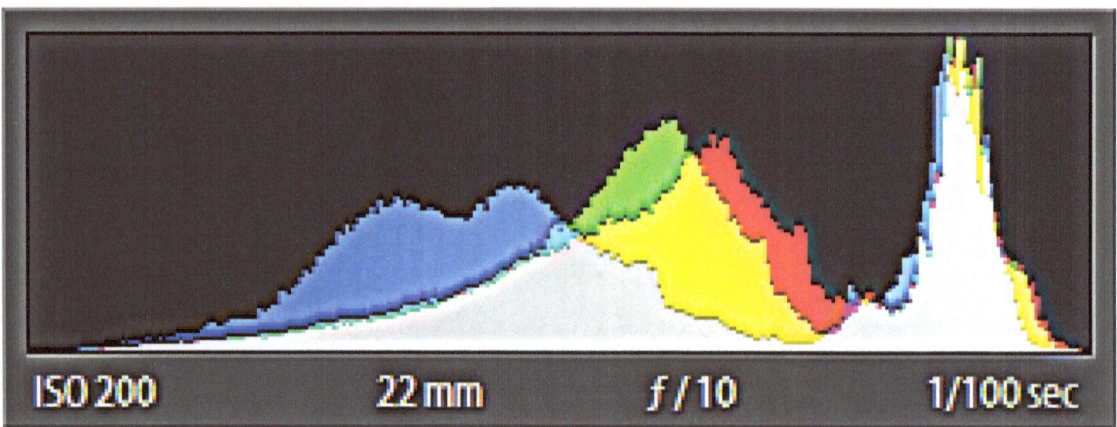

Figure above is too far to the right, meaning the photo is overexposed and the highlights have been blown out.

You can set your camera to show the histogram on your LCD screen with the preview of the photograph that you have just captured to see if the photo has been over- or underexposed or is just right. Look in your camera manual for how to change LCD preview to include the histogram.

You need to watch for clipping of the shadows and highlights. If the histogram graph hills stop at the left side of the histogram the photo is underexposed and you lose shadow details. If the histogram graph hills stop at the right side of the histogram the photo is overexposed and the highlights blown out.

There really is no perfect histogram since the proper exposure for a given photograph may actually be at one extreme based on what you are trying to accomplish. For most photos a good histogram has a bell curve a little to the right of middle. By slightly overexposing your photographs without blowing out the highlights, you can capture more details in the photograph compared to loosing details in the shadows that cannot be recovered.

For most situations, a quick glance at the histogram graph will tell you if your photograph is under- or overexposed.

On some cameras you can see a RGB histogram which is more accurate meter since a basic histogram only shows the overall luminance values. An RGB histogram can show you if a particular RGB color is over- or underexposed. If your camera has the option of displaying an RGB histogram, I recommend that you activate it, see your camera manual for how to do so.

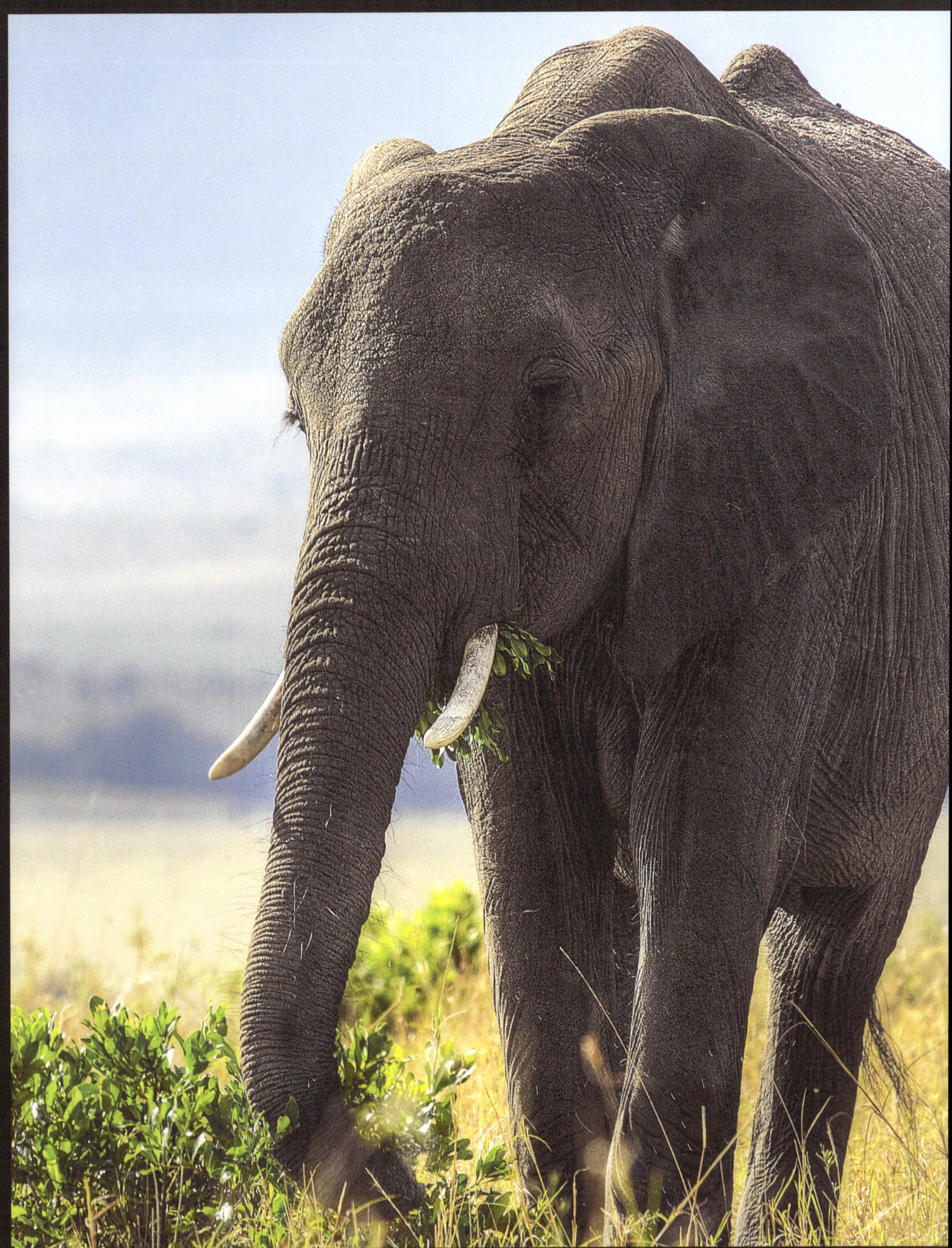

Some cameras also have the ability to turn on overexposure blink. When you see the preview of your photograph on your LCD screen, it will blink in the location where the highlights have been blown out and you are going to lose detail.

To help improve the exposure of your photographs, I really urge you to learn and use the histogram.

Exposure problems

Once you have learned to use the histogram, it is easier to spot exposure problems in your photographs.

A strong over- or underexposed photograph is pretty obvious, too little exposure creates dark tones with little color or detail, and too much exposure results in too bright shadows and blown out highlights.

Underexposed problems:
- Poor color overall.
- Shadows become too deep and loose details.
- Noise becomes more of a problem.

Overexposed problems:
- Weak highlight color.
- Shadows become too dominant due to too much detail.
- Lack of tonal range creates contrast problems.

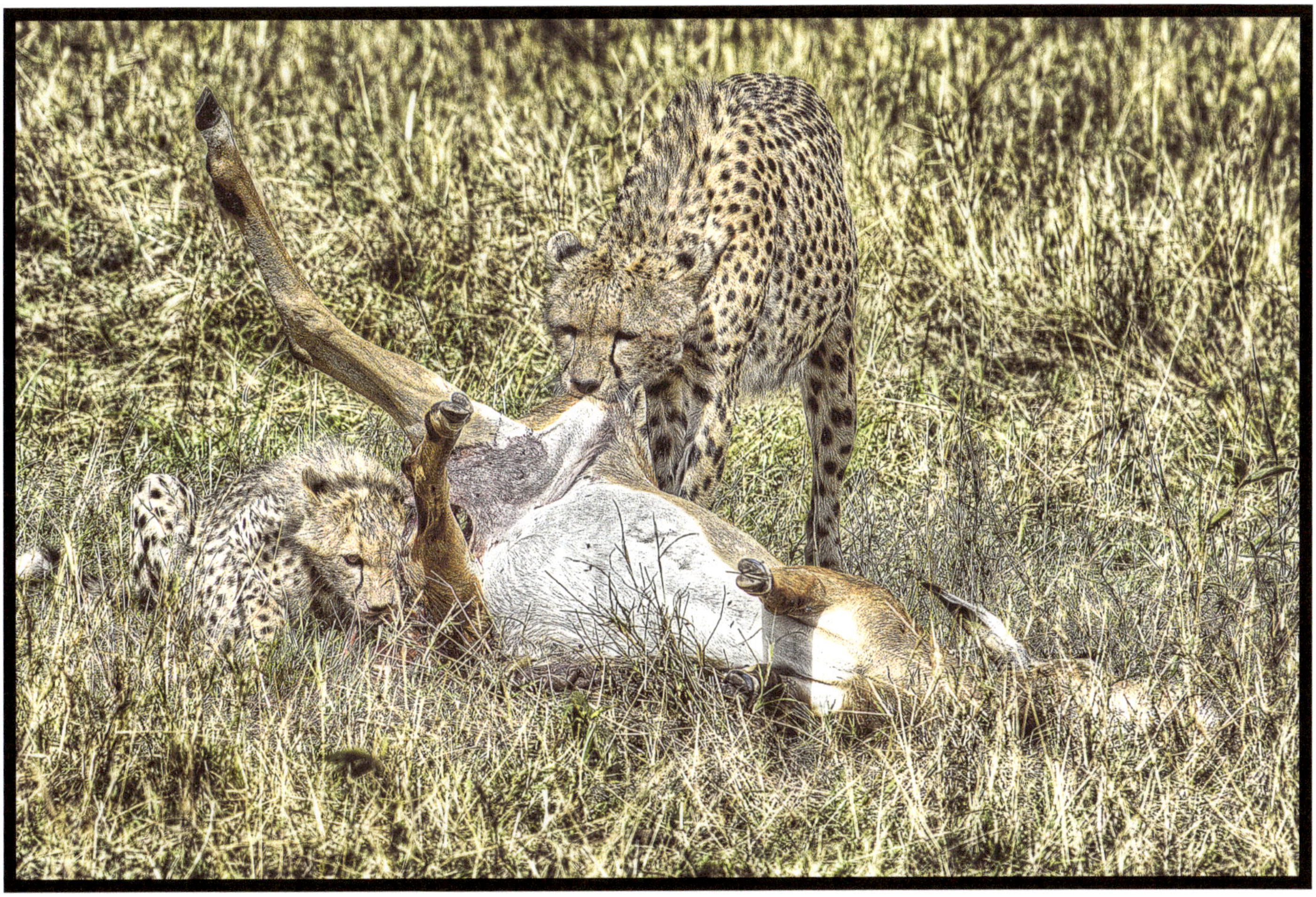

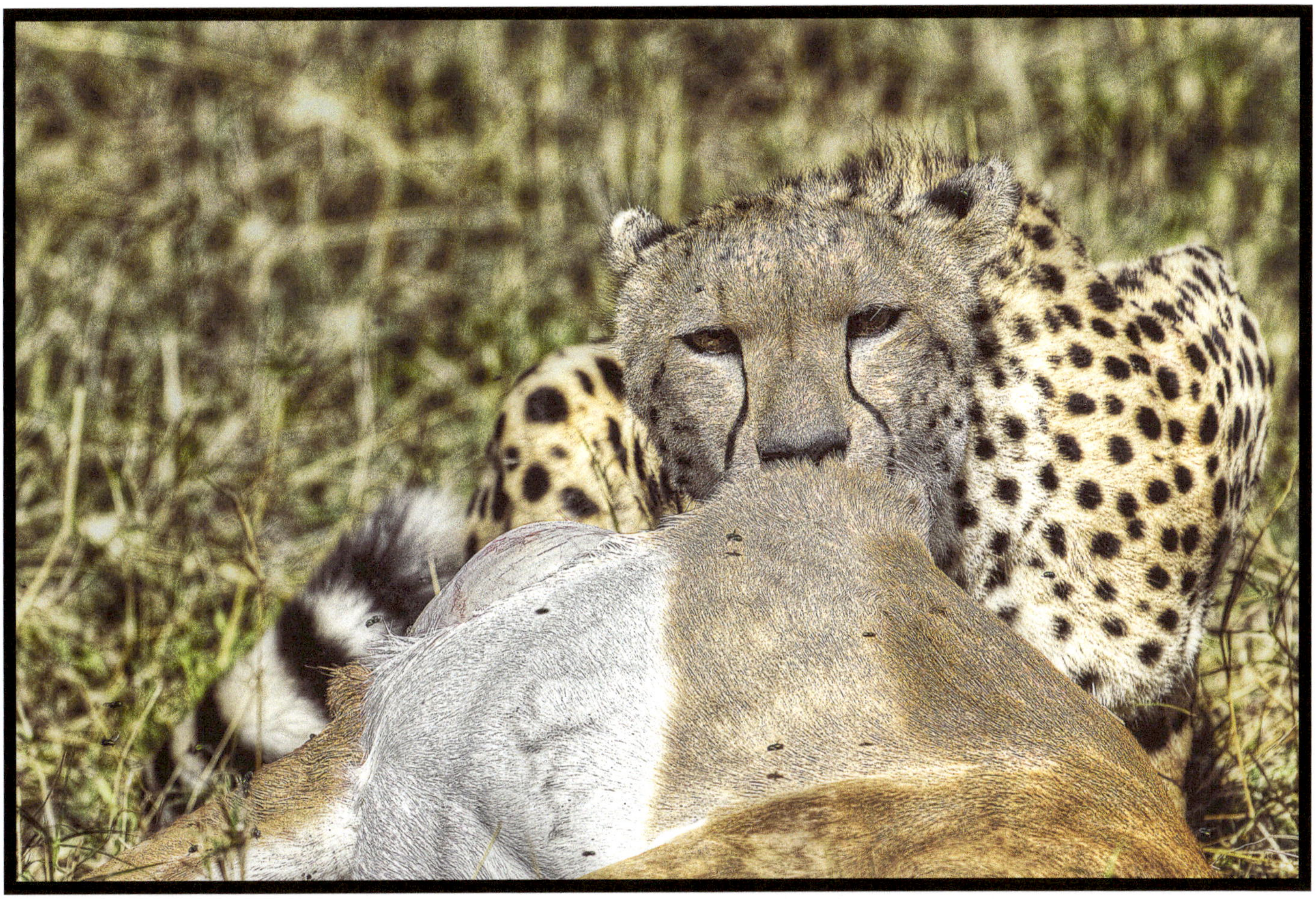

Nature and Wildlife Photography - WorldOfSafari.com

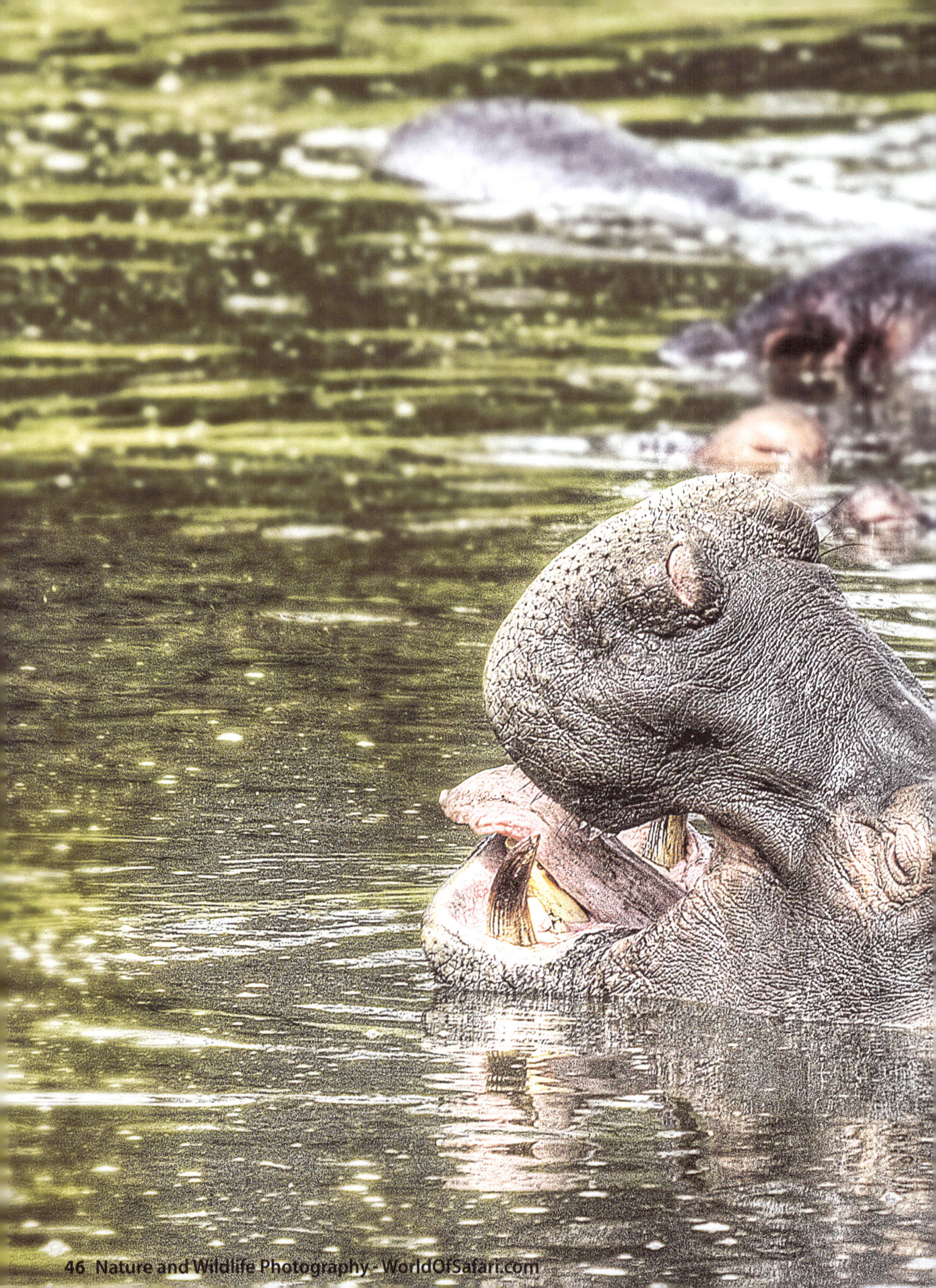

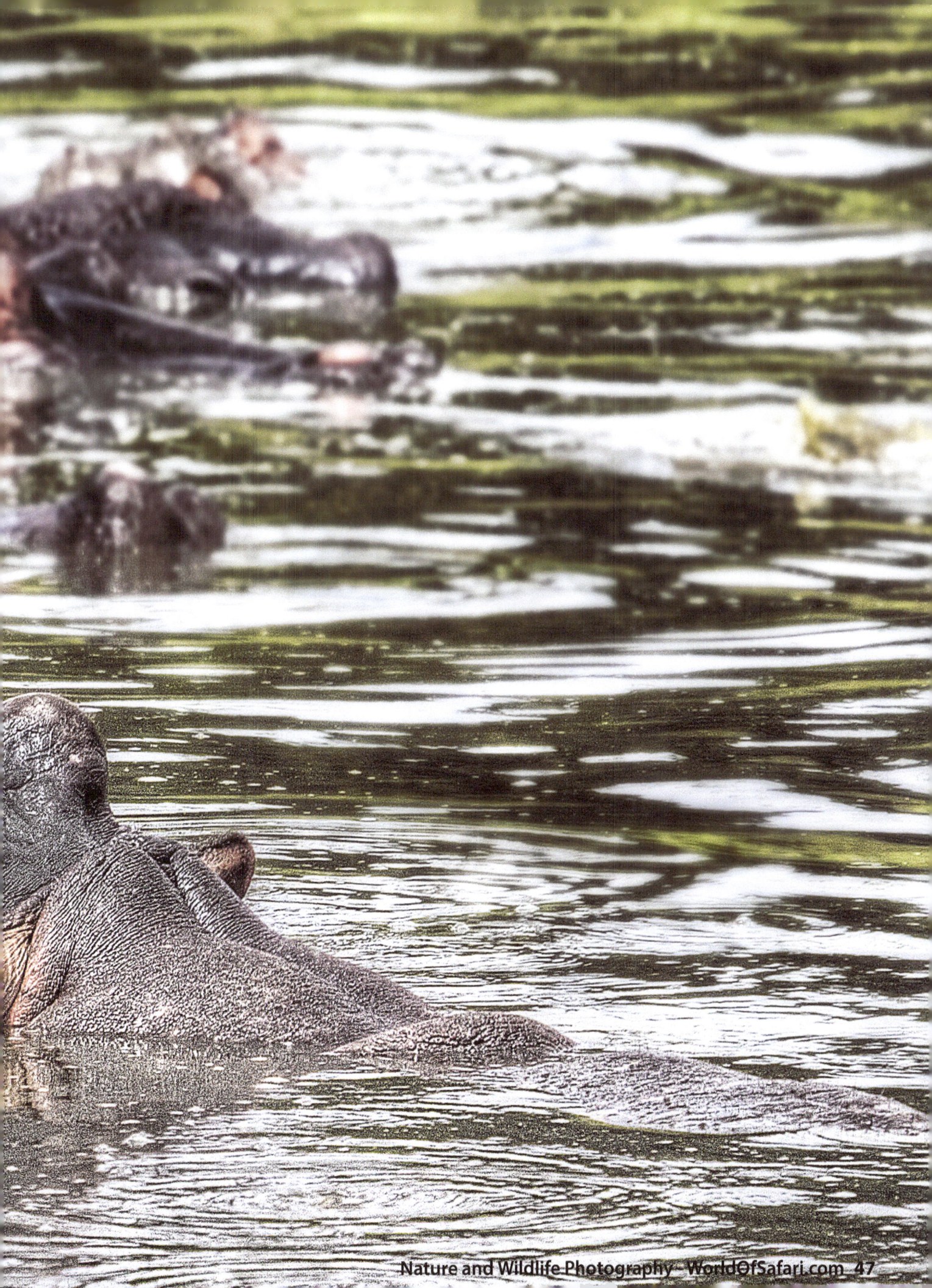

MORE INFORMATION

For more information to an ultimate safari experience go to **www.WorldOfSafari.com** and sign-up for my FREE Newsletter.

Besides information to a safari experience of a life time, my newsletter also includes photography tips and tricks that can instantly improve your safari photos big time no matter the type of camera you are using.

On my website you can also get FREE Safari and Wildlife Apps for Tablets and Mobile Phones.

From the gallery on my website more Safari and Wildlife photos are available in a FREE slideshow for you to enjoy.

Photographs from this book and more are available for purchase from the gallery at my website as high quality prints/photos in different sizes with and without framing delivered directly to you worldwide.

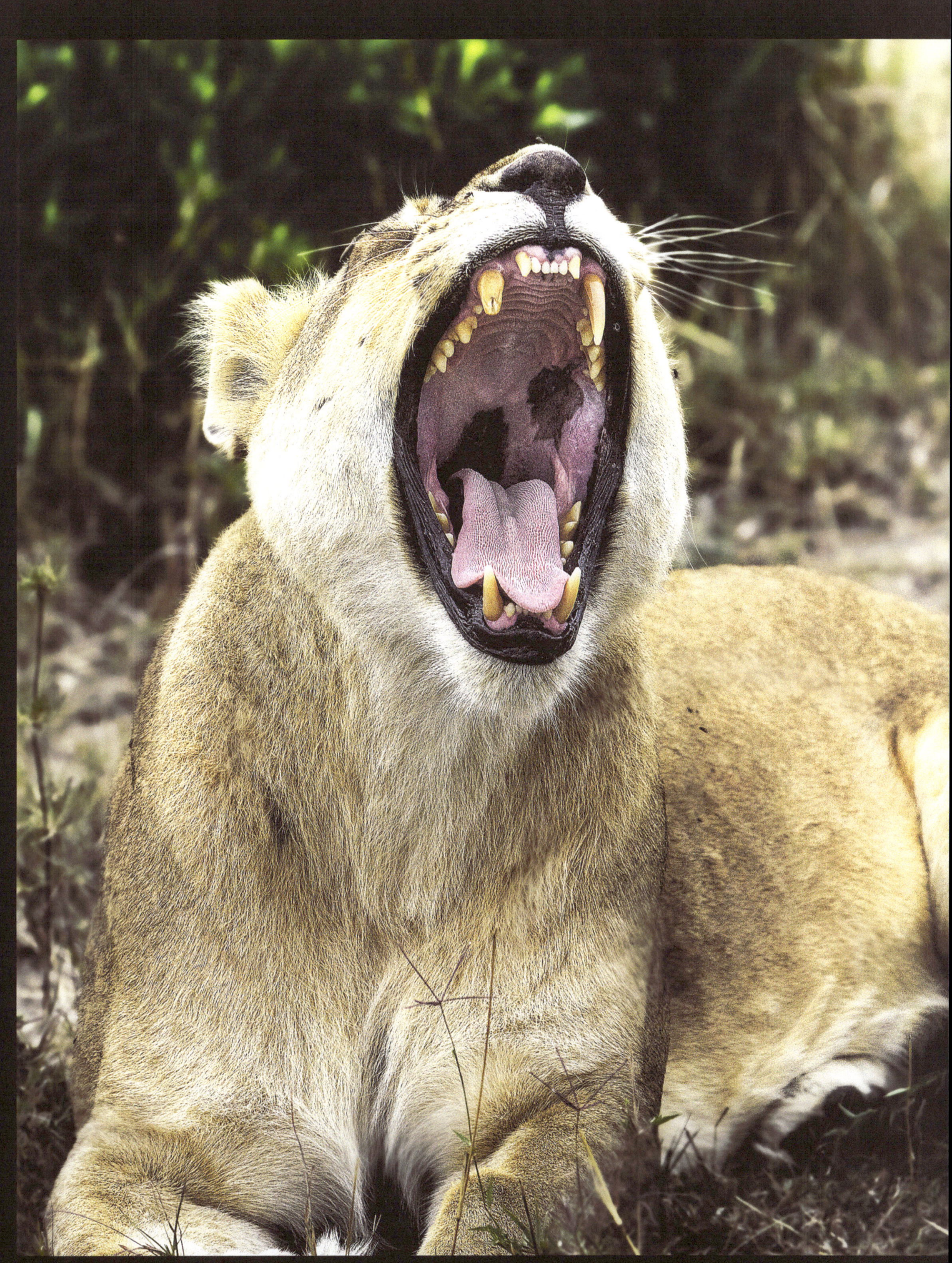

ISBN 978-87-996022-2-3